Data Sovereignty
and
Enterprise Data
Management

Extending Beyond the European Union
General Data Protection Regulation

Sunil Soares
Mark Gallman
Pamela Basil

Information Asset LLC
Harrington Park, NJ
www.information-asset.com

Data Sovereignty and Enterprise Data Management:
Extending Beyond the European Union General Data Protection Regulation
by Sunil Soares, Mark Gallman, and Pamela Basil

First Edition

© Copyright 2017 Information Asset LLC

Information Asset LLC
Harrington Park, NJ • USA
www.information-asset.com

ISBN: 978-0692883051   Printed by CreateSpace

About the Authors

 **Sunil Soares** is the founder and managing partner of Information Asset, a consulting firm that specializes in helping organizations build out their data governance programs. Prior to this role, Sunil was director of information governance at IBM, where he worked with clients across six continents and multiple industries. Before joining IBM, Sunil consulted with major financial institutions at the Financial Services Strategy Consulting Practice of Booz Allen & Hamilton in New York. Sunil lives in New Jersey and holds an MBA in Finance and Marketing from the University of Chicago Booth School of Business.

Sunil is the author of several books, including *The IBM Data Governance Unified Process, Selling Information Governance to the Business: Best Practices by Industry and Job Function, Big Data Governance, IBM InfoSphere: A Platform for Big Data Governance and Process Data Governance, Data Governance Tools, The Chief Data Officer Handbook for Data Governance*, and *Data Governance Guide for BCBS 239 and DFAST Compliance*.

 **Mark Gallman** is a principal consultant with Information Asset. He is experienced in working with clients in developing and operationalizing tailored information governance programs for a number of different industries. He collaborates with cross-functional stakeholders at all levels of the organization in developing best practices, standards, and methodologies to assist in the execution, implementation, and sustainability of governance to support strategic core initiatives. Prior to this role, Mark was a director of financial systems and data governance at CDK Global (formerly ADP Dealer Services), a division of a

Fortune 500 company, specializing in integrated technology and digital marketing solutions to the automotive retail industry and adjacencies. Partnering closely with leaders, Mark developed and directed the strategy for formalized data governance, master data management, and data quality for the organization. Mark has more than 20 years of global experience with large multinational software, manufacturing, and services companies.

Pamela Basil is a manager consultant with Information Asset. Prior to this role, she was vice president of data governance and quality in the chief data office at TD Bank. While at TD Bank, Pam successfully developed and implemented a training program to train more than 350 data stewards, subject matter experts, and data managers. She drove data governance maturity within lines of business across TD Bank and was a key presenter during regulatory examinations of the chief data office.

In a previous role, Pam was supervisor and chief data steward for Independence Blue Cross, a health care payer. Here, she provided leadership and direction to 21 data stewards across the enterprise who managed independent data domains. She led and facilitated enterprise data councils to drive the maturity for corporate reference data.

Pam is a member of DAMA International and vice president of membership on the board of directors for DAMA Philadelphia.

Contents

Preface

Data sovereignty refers to privacy legislation that covers information that is subject to the laws of the country in which the information is located or stored. Data sovereignty laws are emerging as a key inhibitor to cloud-based storage of data. These laws also have an impact when information is created in one country but then is moved to another country for storage, analytics, or processing.

The European Union's General Data Protection Regulation is a recent example of a data sovereignty law. Other examples of data sovereignty legislation include Australia's Privacy Act, Canada's Anti-Spam Law, the People's Republic of China's Cybersecurity Law, and Russia's Personal Data Localization law. As with all enacted regulations, compliance requires a sound data governance program with effective enterprise data management.

Data governance is the formulation of policy to optimize, secure, and leverage information as an enterprise asset by aligning the objectives of multiple functions. By its very nature, data governance boosts cross-departmental cooperation; delivers timely, trustworthy data; and allows all departments to make better decisions.

Enterprise data management refers to the ability of an organization to precisely define, easily integrate, and effectively retrieve data for both internal applications and external communication.[1] It includes a number of disciplines, such as data architecture, data modeling, data integration (extract, transform, load, or ETL), data security, data privacy, master data management, reference data management, data warehousing and business intelligence, information lifecycle management, content management, metadata management, data quality management, data ownership and stewardship, and critical data elements and critical data sets. The terms data governance and enterprise data management are used synonymously in this book.

---

[1] Wikipedia, "Enterprise data management," http://en.wikipedia.org/wiki/Enterprise_
data_management.

This book is geared toward business users and provides a cookbook to operationalize enterprise data management and data governance for data sovereignty compliance. The book includes references to software tools, wherever applicable, and provides insight for the following roles:

- Chief Privacy Officer

- Regulatory Compliance

- Legal

- Internal Audit

- Chief Risk Officer

- Chief Operating Officer

- Chief Information Officer

- Chief Data Officer

- Enterprise Data Management Lead

- Enterprise Information Management Lead

- Data Governance Lead

- Data Steward

- Regulators and Examiners

1

Introduction
to Data Sovereignty

Data sovereignty refers to privacy legislation that covers information that is subject to the laws of the country in which the information is located or stored. Data sovereignty impacts the protection of data, and it is affected by governmental regulations for data privacy, data storage, data processing, and data transfer across international borders. These laws are emerging as a key impediment to cloud-based storage of data, and they need to be fully understood and taken into account when information is created in one country but then moved to another country for storage, analytics, or processing. It is critical to be able to accurately identify who has control and access to the data wherever it is located.

The European Union's (EU's) General Data Protection Regulation (GDPR) is a recent example of a data sovereignty law. The EU published this regulation in May 2016. Following a two-year transition period, the GDPR will go into effect on May 25, 2018. The regulation applies to organizations and data subjects in the European Union. The GDPR applies to the processing of personal data of all data subjects, including customers, employees, and prospects. Non-compliance with the GDPR may result in huge fines, which can be the higher of €20M or 4 percent of the organization's worldwide revenues.

Other examples of data sovereignty legislation include Australia's Privacy Act, Canada's Anti-Spam Law (CASL), the People's Republic of China (PRC) Cybersecurity Law, and Russia's Personal Data Localization law.

The processing of personal data and the protection of electronic communications have become regular topics worldwide and are driving the emergence of data sovereignty legislation changes for ePrivacy. The

European Commission put forward a Proposal for an ePrivacy Regulation on January 10, 2017. The key points of the proposal are:[1]

- *New players*—Privacy rules for electronic communications services such as Facebook® Messenger™, Skype™, and WhatsApp® will guarantee the same level of confidentiality as traditional telecom operators.

- *Stronger rules*—People and businesses will benefit from equal levels of protection of electronic communications that will be sourced to a single set of rules.

- *Communications content and metadata*—Guarantees for privacy of communications content and metadata will require a level of anonymization or destruction dependent upon consent.

- *New business opportunities*—Upon receiving customer consent for processing, additional service opportunities may be developed (e.g., producing heat maps of users to determine where to open a new storefront).

- *Simpler rules on cookies*—Cookie provision will be streamlined to rely on browser settings to track cookie consent or refusal. Clarification in the proposal adds that no consent is needed for non–privacy-intrusive cookies.

- *Protection against spam*—The proposal bans unsolicited electronic communications by email, SMS, and autodial machines.

- *More effective enforcement*—Confidentiality rule enforcement will be the responsibility of data protection authorities in the same way it is under the GDPR.

Data sovereignty regulations exist worldwide and can differ considerably. Obviously, multinational companies are impacted the most by these evolving regulations and must proactively address their needs for compliance. They must either meet the requirements of those countries that have enacted data sovereignty legislation requiring customer data to be processed and kept within the country where the customer resides or follow the letter of the law for allowance and approval to transfer data outside country borders for specific purposes. In some cases, the destina-

---

[1] European Commission, "Proposal for an ePrivacy Regulation," https://ec.europa.eu/digital-single-market/en/proposal-eprivacy-regulation.

tion country may have less restrictive data protection regimes or may have other laws that make it easy for information to land within the public domain. For example, the United States has extensive procedures around legal discovery, such as the U.S. Federal Rules of Civil Procedure, by which personal information pertaining to citizens from other countries may be subject to legal discovery if that data moves to the United States.

Key Terminology

We use some key terms in the book:

Term	Definition
Controller	The natural or legal person, public authority, agency, or other body that, alone or jointly with others, determines the purposes and means of the processing of personal data. Where the purposes and means of such processing are determined by European Union or member state law, the controller or the specific criteria for its nomination may be provided for by Union or member state law.[2]
Personal data	Any information relating to an identified or identifiable natural person ("data subject").[3]
Processor	A natural or legal person, public authority, agency, or other body that processes personal data on behalf of the controller.[4]
Data subject	An identifiable natural person; that is, one who can be identified, directly or indirectly, by reference to an identifier such as a name, an identification number, location data, or an online identifier, or to one or more factors specific to the physical, physiological, genetic, mental, economic, cultural, or social identity of that natural person.[5]
Jurisdiction	A geographic location where regulations may apply.
Critical data	A set of data or information that is necessary to an organization's existence.

Fair Information Practice Principles

At the core of many of today's data privacy laws is the concept of Fair Information Practices (FIPs), a set of principles for protecting the privacy of personal data. In 1973, an advisory committee of the U.S. Department of Health, Education, and Welfare (HEW) published a report entitled *Records, Computers, and the Rights of Citizens: Report of the Secretary's*

---

[2] EU GDPR Article 4, "Definitions," http://www.privacy-regulation.eu/en/4.htm.
[3] Ibid.
[4] Ibid.
[5] Ibid.

Advisory Committee on Automated Personal Data Systems,[6] in which the idea of Fair Information Practices based on a set of core principles for protecting the privacy of personal information in recordkeeping systems was proposed. These Fair Information Practice Principles (FIPPs) became the backbone of the U.S. Privacy Act of 1974, which put in place restrictions limiting the collection, use, and dissemination of personal information held by government agencies. Then, in 1980, the international Organization for Economic Cooperation and Development (OECD) codified its Guidelines on the Protection of Privacy and Transborder Flows of Personal Data.[7] The fair information principles of the HEW report were at the core of the OECD guidelines and were further enhanced to form eight specific principles that were agreed upon by member countries of the OECD (which at that time was a collection of mainly European countries, some Nordic countries, Ireland, the United Kingdom, and the United States). It is these eight FIPPs that have stood as instrumental guidelines in establishing many U.S. and international data privacy standards and data protection regulations.

The eight fair information principles (from the OECD Guidelines on the Protection of Privacy) are listed below:[8]

1. *Collection Limitation Principle*—There should be limits to the collection of personal data, and any such data should be obtained by lawful and fair means and, where appropriate, with the knowledge or consent of the data subject.

2. *Data Quality Principle*—Personal data should be relevant to the purposes for which they are to be used and, to the extent necessary for those purposes, should be accurate, complete, and kept up-to-date.

3. *Purpose Specification Principle*—The purposes for which personal data are collected should be specified not later than at the time of data collection, and the subsequent use limited to the fulfillment of those purposes or such others as are not

---

[6] U.S. Department of Health and Human Services, Office of the Assistant Secretary for Planning and Evaluation, "Records, Computers, and the Rights of Citizens," http://aspe.hhs.gov/DATACNCL/1973privacy/tocprefacemembers.htm.

[7] "OECD Guidelines on the Protection of Privacy and Transborder Flows of Personal Data," http://www.oecd.org/document/18/0,3343,en_2649_34255_1815186_1_1_1_1,00.html.

[8] "OECD Guidelines on the Protection of Privacy and Transborder Flows of Personal Data," http://www.oecd.org/document/18/0,3343,en_2649_34255_1815186_1_1_1_1,00.html, http://www.oecd.org/sti/ieconomy/47683378.pdf.

incompatible with those purposes and as are specified on each occasion of change of purpose.

4. *Use Limitation Principle*—Personal data should not be disclosed, made available, or otherwise used for purposes other than those specified, except with the consent of the data subject or by the authority of law.

5. *Security Safeguards Principle*—Personal data should be protected by reasonable security safeguards against such risks as loss or unauthorized access, destruction, use, modification, or disclosure of data.

6. *Openness Principle*—There should be a general policy of openness about developments, practices, and policies with respect to personal data. Means should be readily available of establishing the existence and nature of personal data, and the main purposes of their use, as well as the identity and usual residence of the data controller.

7. *Individual Participation Principle*—An individual should have the right:

   a. To obtain from a data controller, or otherwise, confirmation of whether or not the data controller has data relating to him;

   b. To have communicated to him, data relating to him within a reasonable time; at a charge, if any, that is not excessive; in a reasonable manner; and in a form that is readily intelligible to him;

   c. To be given reasons if a request made under subparagraphs (a) and (b) is denied, and to be able to challenge such denial; and

   d. To challenge data relating to him and, if the challenge is successful, to have the data erased, rectified, completed, or amended.

8. *Accountability Principle*—A data controller should be accountable for complying with measures that give effect to the principles stated above.

Following are some examples of laws and regulations that use FIPPs to regulate privacy:

- U.S. Federal Trade Commission's Fair Credit Reporting Act
- U.S. Children's Online Privacy and Protection Act (COPPA)
- U.S. Electronic Communications Privacy Act
- U.S. Cable Television Protection and Competition Act

In 1995, the EU adopted Directive 95/46/EC of the European Parliament and of the Council protecting individuals fairly with regard to the processing and movement of their personal data.[9] This directive is the precursor to the EU's General Data Protection Regulation. Many countries created regulations based on the EC directive, so they have inherently adopted the use of FIPPs as well.

Legislation Enforcing Data Privacy and Data Sovereignty

Most countries have implemented and continue to strengthen data privacy laws. Many of these regulations have been enacted as countries have reacted to the need to better safeguard information in the wake of Edward Snowden's revelations about global surveillance programs. Here are a few examples of data sovereignty regulations.

Australia

Australia's Privacy Act of 1988 regulates the handling of personal information about individuals. There are 13 Australian Privacy Principles (APPs), which regulate the collection, use, storage, and disclosure of "personal information" as well as ensure that individuals can access and correct their information. In 2012, Australia introduced the Privacy Amendment (Enhancing Privacy Protection) Act, which gives power to the Office of the Australian Information Commissioner (OAIC), an independent statutory agency, to monitor compliance with privacy policies and the handling of personal information.[10]

---

[9] *Official Journal of the European Communities*, "Directive 95/46/EC of the European Parliament and of the Council of 24 October 1995 on the protection of individuals with regard to the processing of personal data and on the free movement of such data," http://eur-lex.europa.eu/legal-content/EN/TXT/PDF/?uri=CELEX:31995L0046&rid=1.

[10] Office of the Australian Information Commissioner (OAIC), "About Us," https://www.oaic.gov.au/about-us.

European Union

Many EU states have their own current privacy and data protection mandates, which align with the existing EU Directive 95/46/EC. However, the GDPR was enacted to strengthen and unify data protection within the EU, with the primary objectives being to give control back to EU citizens of their personal data and to simplify the regulatory environment for international business through unified regulation.[11]

United States

In August 2016, the EU–U.S. Privacy Shield was adopted to replace Safe Harbor as a compliance framework to protect personal data transfers from the European Union to the United States. While the United States and the European Union share the goal of enhancing privacy protection, the United States takes a different approach to privacy from the EU. The United States uses a sectoral approach that relies on a mix of legislation, regulation, and self-regulation. Given those differences, and to provide organizations in the United States with a reliable mechanism for personal data transfers from the EU while ensuring that EU data subjects continue to benefit from effective safeguards and protection, the U.S. Department of Commerce issued the Privacy Shield Principles.

The Privacy Shield Principles are a set of seven commonly recognized privacy principles (Notice, Choice, Access, Security, Onward Transfer, Data Integrity/Purpose Limitation, and Redress), combined with 16 equally binding supplemental principles that explain and augment the first seven. Collectively, these 23 principles lay out a set of requirements governing participating organizations' use and treatment of personal data received from the EU under the framework, as well as the access and recourse mechanisms that participants must provide to individuals in the EU. Once an organization publicly commits to comply with the Privacy Shield Principles, that commitment is enforceable under U.S. law.[12]

---

[11] Wikipedia, "General Data Protection Regulation," reference 1, https://en.wikipedia.org/wiki/General_Data_Protection_Regulation. "Presidency of the Council: 'Compromise text: Several partial general approaches have been instrumental in converging views in Council on the proposal for a General Data Protection Regulation in its entirety. The text on the Regulation which the Presidency submits for approval as a General Approach appears in annex," 201 pages, 11th June 2015, PDF, http://data.consilium.europa.eu/doc/document/ST-9565-2015-INIT/en/pdf."

[12] Privacy Shield Framework, "Requirements of Participation," https://www.privacyshield.gov/article?id=Requirements-of-Participation.

Russian Federation

In September 2015, Russia's Data Protection Authority, Roskomnadzor, implemented Federal Law 242-FZ (Law 242), a personal data localization law that covers data operators of Russian companies and foreign companies with a presence in Russia that collect personal data about Russian citizens. These operators must initially "record, systematize, accumulate, store, amend, update, retrieve, and extract" data using databases physically located in Russia. Personal data of Russian nationals can still be transferred to foreign databases, but only after having first been processed in Russia and subject to compliance with Russian cross-border transfer rules. Although penalties for noncompliance have not been finalized, they most likely will range from potential fines to, in extreme cases, Roskomnadzor's recommendation to block access to a foreign company's online services (e.g., Roskomnadzor's proposed block of LinkedIn® as a result of that company's failure to transfer Russian user data to data servers physically located in Russia).

China

In November 2016, the People's Republic of China passed the Cybersecurity Law, which takes effect in June 2017. The law has been formulated to ensure network security, preserve cyberspace sovereignty and national security, and to protect the lawful rights and interests of citizens, legal persons, and other organizations. Companies operating in China must store any "personal information and other important data" gathered in-country on servers physically located within mainland China and must employ only technology deemed "secure."[13] Data should not be stored outside the PRC. Any data that needs to be transferred for any business purposes will require governmental permission. Failure to comply with the PRC Cybersecurity Law may result in fines for companies and personally responsible individuals, as well as revoked business licenses, website shutdowns, and other civil and criminal punishments. Organizations should continue to keep an eye out for additional guidance published by Chinese authorities to alleviate the existing uncertainty.

---

[13] China Copyright and Media, "Cybersecurity Law of the People's Republic of China," https://chinacopyrightandmedia.wordpress.com/2016/11/07/cybersecurity-law-of-the-peoples-republic-of-china.

Malaysia

Malaysia's Personal Data Protection Act 2010 (Act 709) supports seven Personal Data Protection Principles: the General Principle, the Notice and Choice Principle, the Disclosure Principle, the Security Principle, the Retention Principle, the Data Integrity Principle, and the Access Principle.[14] Sections 47 and 48 of the Malaysia Personal Data Protection Act ("Appointment of commissioner" and "Functions of commissioner") introduce and give power to a Personal Data Protection Commissioner. The commissioner position was established to advise the minister on personal data protection national policy and related matters and to monitor, implement, and enforce the personal data protection laws while encouraging associations representing data users to develop policy and guidelines to comply with the act. The act specifies that personal data shall not be transferred to places outside Malaysia unless the minister has determined that the place has substantial data protection regulations in relation to the processing of personal data.[15]

Germany

The German Federal Data Protection Act was published on January 14, 2003, with an amendment to the act in August 2009. The act, which implements a directive of the European Parliament (94/46/EC), is designed to protect individuals and their privacy. The regulation covers data that is collected, consented to, processed, stored, destroyed, transferred, and used.[16] In Germany, the Bundestag, one of two legislative chambers of the Federal Republic of Germany, elects the Federal Commissioner for Data Protection and Freedom of Information, who is then appointed into office by the Federal President. The commissioner is required to monitor compliance, including investigating data protection matters on behalf of the public.[17] The Bundestag mandates that the commissioner produce a report of activities in the field of data protection every two years.[18] The Data Protection Act separates personal data transfers into categories based on where the data is going geographically, whether consent was provided by the data subjects, and whether transfers require notification. Personal data transferred to areas outside the Euro-

---

[14] The Law of Malaysia Personal Data Protection Act, Act 709, Section 5 (1)(a-g), http://www.pdp.gov.my/images/LAWS_OF_MALAYSIA_PDPA.pdf.

[15] The Law of Malaysia Personal Data Protection Act, Act 709, Section 129.

[16] Translation of the German Federal Data Protection Act, https://www.gesetze-im-internet.de/englisch_bdsg/englisch_bdsg.html.

[17] German Federal Data Protection Act, Chapter III, Sections 22–26.

[18] German Federal Data Protection Act, Chapter III, Section 26.

pean Union or member states will require that the destination country has sufficient data protection regulations in place and data subject consent.

Hong Kong

Hong Kong, China, has published a Personal Data (Privacy) Ordinance (Chapter 486) that provides guidance for the protection of individuals in relation to personal data as well as providing for the management of incidents. The ordinance was published June 30, 1997, with several editorial updates to maintain currency. The office of Privacy Commissioner for Personal Data was established because of the ordinance. The chief executive is accountable for appointing the commissioner, who may hold the position for five years with only one additional five-year term. The commissioner is responsible for monitoring and supervising compliance with the provisions of the ordinance.[19] The ordinance provides guidance for adhering to the Data Protection Principles,[20] ensuring the rights of data subjects and enforcing consequences for failing to comply with the ordinance. The ordinance contains specific guidance related to the transfer of personal data to places outside Hong Kong. Personal data that has been collected, stored, or processed in Hong Kong or is controlled by an organization whose principal place of business is within Hong Kong shall not transfer personal data to places outside Hong Kong, with exceptions for transfers to places with substantially similar laws as found within the ordinance.[21]

Singapore

Singapore's Personal Data Protection Act 2012 was assented to by the President, Tony Tan Keng Yam, on November 20, 2012. The act was created to aid in the governance of the collection, use, and disclosure of personal data by organizations as well as to establish a Do Not Call Register. The purpose of the act, while providing governance, also recognizes the rights of individuals to protect their personal data and the need of organizations to collect, use, or disclose personal data for appropriate practices. The act is administered by the Personal Data Protection Commission, which also promotes awareness across the country for data protection, serves as an advisor, and represents the

---

[19] Hong Kong Personal Data (Privacy) Ordinance (Chapter 486), Section 6, http://www.blis. gov.hk/blis_pdf.nsf/CurAllEngDoc/B4DF8B4125C4214D482575EF000EC5FF/$FILE/ CAP_486_e_b5.pdf.

[20] Hong Kong Personal Data (Privacy) Ordinance (Chapter 486), Schedule 1.

[21] Hong Kong Personal Data (Privacy) Ordinance (Chapter 486), Section 33.

government internationally on data protection matters.[22] Section 26 of Part VI of the Personal Data Protection Act states that organizations shall not transfer any personal data to a country or territory outside Singapore unless the commission allows an exemption.

Switzerland

The Federal Act on Data Protection for the Swiss Confederation was published on June 19, 1992, and was updated as late as January 1, 2014. The goal of the act is to protect the privacy and fundamental rights of persons when their data is processed. Five principles for general data protection are set out within Section 2, Article 4, of the act:

- Personal data may only be processed lawfully.

- Its processing must be carried out in good faith and must be proportionate.

- Personal data may only be processed for the purpose indicated at the time of collection, that is evident from the circumstances, or that is provided for by law.

- The collection of personal data, and in particular the purpose of its processing, must be evident to the data subject.

- If the consent of the data subject is required for the processing of personal data, such consent is valid only if given voluntarily on the provision of adequate information. Consent must be given expressly in the case of processing of sensitive personal data or personality profiles.[23]

Data sovereignty is highlighted in the act's Article 6 (Cross-border disclosure). This article states that personal data may not be disclosed abroad if the privacy of the data subject would be seriously endangered or if the receiving area does not have sufficient legislation to guarantee adequate protection. Section 5 of the act provides guidance about the appointment, status, and tasks of the Federal Data Protection and Information Commissioner, who is appointed to a four-year term by the Federal Council.

---

[22] Singapore Personal Data Protection Act 2012, Part I, Section 3, and Part II, Sections 5 and 6, http://statutes.agc.gov.sg/aol/search/display/view.w3p;page=0;query=DocId%3Aea8b8b45-51b8-48cf-83bf-81d01478e50b%20Depth%3A0%20Status%3Ainforce;rec=0.

[23] Federal Act on Data Protection, Federal Assembly of the Swiss Confederation, Section 2, General Data Protection Provisions, Article 4, Principles 1–5, https://www.admin.ch/opc/en/classified-compilation/19920153/index.html#.

Argentina

Enacted on October 4, 2000, the Argentina Personal Data Protection Act 25.326 is designed to serve as a comprehensive protection of personal information that may exist in recorded files, records, databases, data banks, or other technical mechanisms. The act, a supporting document to the National Constitution, applies to both public and private organizations that may produce reports or access personal data. While a few exceptions are stated, the Personal Data Protection Act prohibits the transfer of any type of personal information to other countries or to international or supranational entities that do not possess adequate levels of protection.[24] To ensure compliance with the act, the National Executive Power established a controlling body, or Controlling Agency. The Controlling Agency's functions and powers include performing a census of data files, registers, or banks covered by the act and keeping permanent records thereof.[25]

Poland

The Act of August 29, 1997, on the Protection of Personal Data in the Republic of Poland was last updated June 1, 2016. This regulation applies to the processing of personal data in files, indexes, books, lists, and other registers and computer systems. The act provides direction on the collection, consent, processing, erasure, integrity, transfer, and monitoring of personal data. The Inspector General for Personal Data Protection, in conjunction with controllers, and appointed administrators of information security are responsible for protecting the rights of the data subjects and ensuring that organizations take necessary steps to implement technical and organizational measures to protect the personal data being processed, appropriate to the risks and category of data being protected.[26] Article 47 of Chapter 7 (Transfer of personal data to a third country) gives organizations guidance for acceptable transfers. This article states that transfers outside the Republic of Poland may occur only if the destination ensures at least the same level of personal data protection within its territory.[27]

---

[24] Argentina Personal Data Protection Act 25.326, http://unpan1.un.org/intradoc/groups/public/documents/un-dpadm/unpan044147.pdf.

[25] Argentina Personal Data Protection Act 25.326, Chapter V, Section 29(1).

[26] Republic of Poland, Act of August 29, 1997, on the Protection of Personal Data, Chapter 5, Article 36, www.giodo.gov.pl/plik/id_p/248/j/en.

[27] Republic of Poland, Act of August 29, 1997, on the Protection of Personal Data, Chapter 7, Article 47.

South Korea

South Korea's Personal Information Protection Act (PIPA) went into effect September 30, 2011. The act has been designed to enhance the rights and interests of citizens and to protect their privacy from unauthorized collection, abuse, misuse, or leakage.[28] The act addresses eight Personal Information Protection Principles and provides instructions for processing, collection, consent by data subjects, integrity, anonymity, and responsibilities of data processors. The Presidential Office of South Korea has established a Personal Information Protection Commission to independently resolve any matters related to the improvement of policies, systems, and legislation related to data protection as well as matters related to privacy impact assessments.[29] The act also refers processors to guidelines for destruction of personal data, use of visual data processing devices, and transfers. In addition to the commission, the act provides guidance for organizations to designate a privacy officer who will oversee personal information processing and take necessary corrective action in the event of a violation of the act. Transfers of personal information within South Korea and to international environments outside South Korea are permitted only if proper international cooperation is achieved and data subject rights are not infringed upon,[30] when the organization obtains consent prior to transferring personal information to a third party overseas,[31] if data subjects are notified,[32] and when organizations provide advance notification to data subjects when the transfer is related to business.[33]

Enterprise Data Management and Data Governance

Enterprise data management (EDM) refers to the ability of an organization to precisely define, easily integrate, and effectively retrieve data for both internal applications and external communication.[34] It includes a

---

[28] Personal Information Protection Act, Article 1, "Purpose," http://koreanlii.or.kr/w/images/0/0e/KoreanDPAct2011.pdf.

[29] Personal Information Protection Act, Article 8, "Functions of the Commission."

[30] Personal Information Protection Act, Article 14, "International Cooperation."

[31] Personal Information Protection Act, Article 17(3), "Provision of Personal Information."

[32] Personal Information Protection Act, Article 27(1), "Limitation to Transfer of Personal Information following Business Transfer, etc."

[33] Personal Information Protection Act, Article 27(2), "Limitation to Transfer of Personal Information following Business Transfer, etc."

[34] Wikipedia, "Enterprise data management," http://en.wikipedia.org/wiki/Enterprise_data_management.

number of disciplines, such as data architecture, data modeling, data integration (extract, transform, load, or ETL), data security, data privacy, master data management, reference data management, data warehousing and business intelligence, information lifecycle management, content management, metadata management, data quality management, data ownership and stewardship, and critical data elements (CDEs) and critical data sets. Strictly speaking, data security and privacy are broader disciplines, but they have significant interdependencies with enterprise data management and data governance.

The terms data governance and enterprise data management are used synonymously in this book.

As shown in Figure 1.1, data governance is a foundational program that ties together the other EDM disciplines.

Figure 1.1: The EDM disciplines that contribute to comprehensive data governance

We discuss each EDM discipline below:

- *Data governance*—The formulation of policy to optimize, secure, and leverage information as an enterprise asset by aligning the objectives of multiple functions.

- *Data architecture*—A discipline that sets data standards for data systems as a vision or a model of the eventual interactions between those data systems.[35]

- *Data modeling*—The process of establishing data models, which use a set of symbols and text to precisely explain a subset of real information to improve communication within the organization and thereby lead to a more flexible and stable application environment.[36]

- *Data integration*—A process that involves combining data from multiple sources to provide new insights to business users.

- *Data security*—The process of avoiding unauthorized access to data.

- *Data privacy*—The process that involves protecting data that belongs to an individual or organization. Privacy is the "right to be left alone," as defined in a *Harvard Law Review* article called "The Right to Privacy" written in 1890 by Justice Louis Brandeis and Samuel Warren.[37] Subsequent regulations and legislation around the world have built on this definition.

- *Master data management*—The process of establishing a single version of the truth for an organization's critical data entities, such as customers, products, materials, vendors, and chart of accounts.

- *Reference data management*—The process of managing static data such as country codes, state or province codes, and industry classification codes, which may be placed in lookup tables for reference by other applications across the enterprise.

---

[35] Wikipedia, "Data architecture," http://en.wikipedia.org/wiki/Data_architecture.
[36] Steve Hoberman, *Data Modeling Made Simple*, 2nd Edition (Technics Publications LLC, 2009).
[37] Susan E. Gallagher, "Context," http://faculty.uml.edu/sgallagher/harvard__law_review.htm.

- *Data warehousing and business intelligence*—The process of creating a centralized repository of data for reporting and analysis.

- *Information lifecycle management*—The process and methodology of managing information through its lifecycle, from creation through disposal, including compliance with legal, regulatory, and privacy requirements.

- *Content management*—The process of digitizing, collecting, and classifying paper and electronic documents.

- *Metadata management*—The management of information that describes the characteristics of any data artifact, such as its name, location, criticality, quality, business rules, and relationships to other data artifacts.

- *Data quality management*—A discipline that includes methods to measure and improve the quality and integrity of an organization's data.

- *Data ownership and stewardship*—The process of identifying individuals who will be accountable for the trustworthiness, as well as supporting security and privacy, of data within their purview.

- *Critical data elements and critical data sets*—In the context of data sovereignty, critical data elements and critical data sets (groupings or collections of data) are data that may cause operational, regulatory, or financial risk if they are not collected or are incorrect, compromised, or used inappropriately.

The key EDM disciplines for data sovereignty compliance are data architecture (taxonomy), data ownership, critical data elements and critical data sets, metadata management, data security, and data privacy.

Operationalizing Enterprise Data Management for Global Data Sovereignty

Successful data sovereignty requires collaboration across the organization, including among those responsible for legal, risk, compliance, information technology, and enterprise data management. The amalgamation of skills and technology within the organization will support the operationalization. Figure 1.2 depicts the 16 steps to comply with data sovereignty based on data governance.

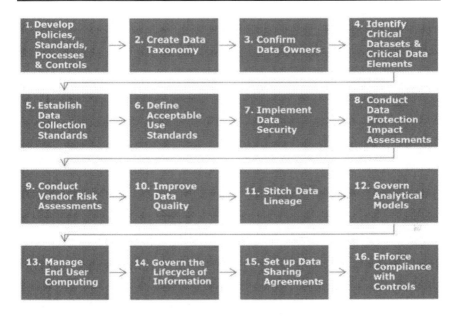

Figure 1.2: End-to-end approach to operationalize data governance for data sovereignty

1. Develop Policies, Standards, Processes, and Controls

A strong enterprise data management program is the first step in facilitating data sovereignty compliance. Data governance programs should establish policies, standards, processes, and controls to support compliance with data privacy and sovereignty regulations. Figure 1.3 illustrates a consistent data collection policy. The policy is supported by data standards pertaining to consistent customer data collection, consent to customer communication, and customer notification of data use at collection. Data processes provide detailed instructions on how customers must be given the choice as to how they prefer to be contacted by organizations for marketing purposes. Finally, data controls provide an enforcement mechanism to ensure that the organization complies with processes. These controls operate on critical data such as email opt-in, do not email, and email opt-out, and they operationalize CASL Section 6.1, APP 7, and GDPR Article 7. We'll define these concepts further in Chapter 2.

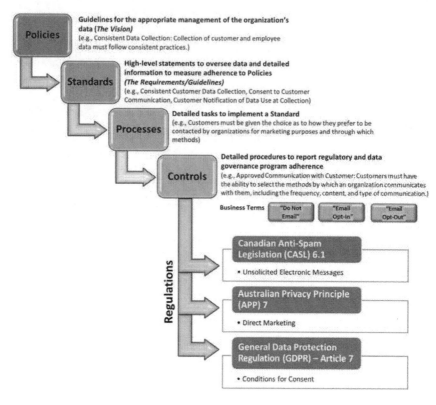

Figure 1.3: Data management hierarchy through regulatory compliance, a four-tiered approach

2. Create Data Taxonomy

The data governance team needs to collaborate with the enterprise data architecture team to classify data into categories and subcategories. This helps to build a holistic picture of all the data that the organization needs to govern from a data sovereignty perspective. In Figure 1.4, customer data is shown at the very highest level and then is classified further by country.

Figure 1.4: Sample taxonomy for global customer data

3. Confirm Data Owners

The next step is to define data owners who are ultimately accountable for one or more data categories and subcategories. These data owners will appoint data stewards who will be accountable for day-to-day operations regarding the data. The data stewards will be responsible for identifying critical data sets and critical data elements as well as establishing standards, including standards for data collection, acceptable use, and data masking in conjunction with enterprise data management, legal, privacy, and compliance.

4. Identify Critical Data Sets and Critical Data Elements

The 16-step process implies that an organization will require rigorous data governance exercises. Data stewards should prioritize their efforts by identifying critical data sets and critical data elements within their respective data categories. If we look back to the example regarding customer, a customer's identity will consist of multiple CDEs that will require data sovereignty needs, including name, gender, address, email address, postal code, date of birth, and customer ID. The data governance team needs to work in conjunction with legal and compliance teams to determine whether standards for data collection and use are best set at the level of critical data set rather than at the individual CDE level. In Figure 1.5, taxonomy and data ownership are tied together by the identification of critical data elements within the category of customer.

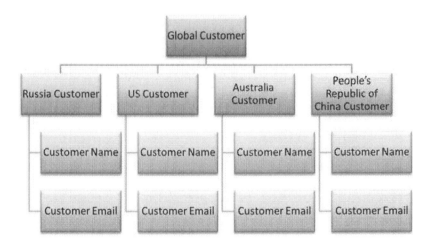

Figure 1.5: CDE ownership based on taxonomy

5. Establish Data Collection Standards

Some regulations require organizations to implement appropriate technical and organizational measures to ensure that only personal data that is necessary for the specific purpose of the processing is processed. Article 25 of the GDPR (Data protection by design and by default) and Australian Privacy Principal 3 (Collection of solicited personal information) are two examples of regulations where these obligations apply to the amount of personal data collected, the extent of their processing, the period of their storage, and their accessibility. The data governance team must establish controls so that legal and compliance sign off on data collection for any new project during the ideation phase. As an example, a software company may use an online form to allow users to download software on a trial basis. In this scenario, it would be reasonable for the form to request the applicant's name and email address; however, it would be inappropriate for the company to also request the applicant's date of birth and national identifier.

6. Define Acceptable Use and Security Standards

Several data sovereignty regulations, including the EU GDPR, Singapore Personal Data Protection Act (PDPA), Australian Privacy Act of 1988, and the Canada Personal Information Protected and Electronic Documents Act (PIPEDA), require that organizations, or controllers of data, demonstrate that consent was provided by data subjects to process personal data. Data governance and management teams must work with technology, legal, and compliance to establish an enterprise consent repository. The enterprise consent repository must contain an immutable record of consent from data subjects. For example, the repository may contain a record of consent from users of the company's website to the use of web cookies. The data governance team must establish controls to ensure that any new projects that require the use of personal data achieve signoff by legal and compliance during the ideation phase.

7. Implement Data Security

Australian Privacy Principle 2 refers to anonymity and pseudonymity. Data subjects must have the option to not identify themselves, or to use a pseudonym, when dealing with organizations. Article 32 of the GDPR deals with the security of processing. Considering the state of the art, the costs of implementation, and the nature, scope, context, and purposes of processing, as well as the risk of varying likelihood and severity for the rights and freedoms of natural persons, the controller and the processor shall implement appropriate technical and organizational measures to ensure a level of security appropriate to the risk. The data governance office must establish controls to appropriately mask or encrypt sensitive personal data. The data masking standards need to ensure that data cannot be reconstructed when multiple fields are combined.

8. Conduct Data Protection Impact Assessments

Several data sovereignty laws, such as the GDPR and the Irish Data Protection Acts of 1998 and 2003, have instituted formal requirements for data protection impact assessments. According to Article 35 of the GDPR, a data protection impact assessment is an assessment of the impact of processing operations on the protection of personal data. The GDPR states that the controller shall carry out a data protection impact assessment where a type of processing uses new technologies or is likely to result in a high risk to the rights and freedoms of natural persons. Privacy impact assessment is a term that is often used synonymously with data protection impact assessment.

9. Conduct Vendor Risk Assessments

There will always be a risk associated with having data outside the company. Vendor risk assessments facilitate a process of evaluating the level of protection and adherence to increasing regulatory requirements for the processing, treatment, and management of personal data carried out by others on behalf of controllers. Risk assessments focus on a number of areas, including data storage, transmissions/transfers across borders, access to data, security practices, data loss prevention (DLP), disaster recovery, and data segregation in the cloud. There are some tools on the market today to help assess the risk of partnering with vendors. These tools perform these tasks in an automated fashion. The role of data governance teams in these activities is more consultative, while the legal, risk, and compliance teams may take on more of the responsible and accountable roles.

10. Improve Data Quality

Article 16 of the GDPR (Right to rectification) requires companies to rectify inaccurate personal information and address incomplete personal data without undue delay. Data governance teams need to establish controls to allow customers, employees, and other data subjects to address any data quality issues relating to their personal information in a timely manner. Section 22 of the Hong Kong Personal Data Privacy Ordinance (Chapter 486) not only requires data users to make corrections to data subject–identified inaccuracies, but stipulates that the data user has an obligation to ensure that if said data was transferred to a third party, the third-party data user must also make the requested corrections.

11. Stitch Data Lineage

Article 30 of the GDPR requires organizations to maintain a record of processing activities. This record must include a description of the categories of personal data, the categories of recipients of personal data (including those in third countries or international organizations), and transfers of personal data to a third country or to an international organization. The recordkeeping requirements also extend to so-called processors who process data on behalf of an organization. To comply with this article, data governance teams need to strengthen metadata management and data lineage capabilities. For example, the data lineage for customer information needs to include the movement from application A to application B within the organization, as well as the transfer to the outsourcer and to its subcontractor (Figure 1.6).

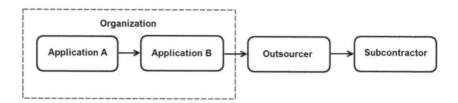

Figure 1.6: Data lineage for customer information from organization to outsourcer and subcontractor

12. Govern Analytical Models

Data scientists build models for various purposes, including predictive analytics and risk management. These analytical models should also be governed in a manner similar to CDEs and data standards. At a minimum, data governance teams need to build a model inventory that includes the model name, model owner, input variables, output variables, model methodology, creation date, and completed or planned validation activities. Article 22 of the GDPR addresses automated individual decision-making, including profiling. Additional regulations, such as the PRC's Cybersecurity Law, require that personal information be stored, handled, and analyzed within the territory of China and not shared or transferred overseas, including for analytical purposes. As organizations engage in data analytics, there are U.S. federal equal opportunity laws to consider, such as the Equal Credit Opportunity Act, the Fair Credit Reporting Act, and the Americans with Disabilities Act. These laws prohibit discrimination based on protected characteristics such as race, color, sex or gender, religion, age, disability status, national origin, marital status, and genetic information. Using analytics based on these characteristics may cause a disparate impact, which may often run afoul of these regulations.

13. Manage End User Computing

Article 32 of the GDPR addresses the security of processing personal data, Australian Privacy Principle 11 addresses the security of personal information, and Singapore's Personal Data Protection Act 24 addresses the protection of personal data. Organizations typically generate a significant volume of end user computing (EUC) applications in the form of spreadsheets and databases that may be stored on desktops or in Microsoft® SharePoint® repositories. EUCs are typically outside the control of IT and often contain sensitive personal data. The data governance team must establish a repository of EUCs including the name of the application, owner, description of sensitive data, and creation date. The data governance team must establish controls to ensure that EUC owners update the repository on a regular basis and conduct an annual validation exercise for existing EUCs.

14. Govern the Lifecycle of Information

Article 17 of the GDPR provides for the right to erasure, commonly known as the "right to be forgotten." Data subjects may require companies to erase their personal data in several situations, including when the information is no longer necessary in relation to the purpose for which it was originally collected. Data governance teams need to establish mechanisms to allow data subjects to request the erasure of their data. These teams must also establish operational controls so that such requests are reviewed and acted on in a timely manner. A metadata repository is key to quickly identifying all the places where a person's data resides within the organization or its processors.

15. Set Up Data Sharing and Movement Agreements

Australian Privacy Principle 1.3–1.4 states that entities must have policies that clearly define whether personal information is likely to be disclosed to overseas recipients and must state in which countries the recipients may be located. Australian Privacy Principle 8.1 addresses an entity's requirement to validate that an overseas recipient of personal information does not violate the principles. Section 26(1) of Singapore's Personal Data Protection Act provides instructions for transfers of personal data, including requirements to ensure that stringent personal data protection standards are met when data is moved outside Singapore. The data governance team must ensure that the legal and compliance teams sign off on data sharing agreements prior to any movement of personal data from within one country to outside that country, from an organization within a country to a vendor, and from a vendor to a downstream processor.

16. Enforce Compliance with Data Sovereignty Controls

Regulatory controls are a key component of an overall framework to support compliance. The data governance team must establish a framework for regulatory controls. Internal audit, legal, and compliance teams can enforce the adherence and compliance with these controls on an ongoing basis.

Summary

Data sovereignty laws will become increasingly important to multinationals with business operations, customers, and employees in several countries. We have outlined 16 core steps to operationalize a data governance program geared to data sovereignty compliance. The order and importance of each step may vary based on each organization's needs and existing data governance structure. Data security and privacy are imperative to the success of the organization.

2

Policy, Standards, Processes, and Controls

Regulation sample	Description
Canada's Anti-Spam Law, Provision 44	Directors and officers of corporations— "An officer, director, agent, or mandatary of a corporation that commits an offense is a party to and liable for the offense if they directed, authorized, assented to, acquiesced in, or participated in the commission of the offense, whether or not the corporation is proceeded against."
Australian Privacy Act of 1988, Principle 1, Subclause 1.3	Open and transparent management of personal information— "An APP entity must have a clearly expressed and up-to-date policy (the APP privacy policy) about the management of personal information by the entity."
European Union General Data Protection Regulation, Article 7(1)	Conditions for consent— ". . .the controller shall be able to demonstrate that the data subject has consented to processing of his or her personal data."
California Law, Division 3, Part 4, Title 1.8. Personal Data [1798–1798.78], Chapter 1, Article 7	Accounting of disclosures [1798.25–1798.29]— ". . .Any agency that owns or licenses computerized data that includes personal information shall disclose any breach of the security of the system following discovery or notification of the breach in the security of the data to any resident of California. . . ."

The first step in the data governance journey is to formulate data governance policies and standards. A data governance playbook is a guide that allows organizations to establish a framework to manage data policies, standards, processes, and controls. These artifacts may be found in many places, including in people's heads or embedded in broader policy manuals. Some organizations document their policies in Microsoft Word® or PowerPoint® and load the documents to SharePoint or an intranet portal.

Prescribe Terminology for Data Policies

Several terms—such as policies, standards, processes, guidelines, and principles—are used to describe data decisions. Organizations must use consistent terminology to describe these decisions. In this book, we use a standard framework of data policies, standards, processes, and controls. We begin this chapter by defining these key terms:

Term	Definition
Data policies	These provide a broad framework for how decisions should be made regarding data. Data policies are guidelines for the appropriate management of an organization's data. One or more data standards may support each data policy.
Data standards	These are high-level statements and need more detail before they can be operationalized. They provide detailed rules about how to implement data policies. One or more data processes may support each data standard.
Data processes	These provide detailed tasks to implement a standard and include special instructions for the successful implementation of data standards.
Data controls	These provide detailed procedures to report regulatory and data governance program adherence. One or more regulations may support each data standard and policy; multiple business terms may also be regulated by these controls.

Data Security Policy

Figure 2.1 shows a hierarchy of policy, standards, processes, and controls for the data security policy "Support primary security objectives of organization." The data policy is supported by data standards pertaining to data breach notifications. Data processes provide detailed instructions about how notification must be made to data subjects and to authorities. Finally, data controls provide an enforcement mechanism to ensure that the organization complies with processes. These controls operationalize California Law, Division 3, Part 4, Title 1.8, 1798.29; GDPR Article 33; and GDPR Article 34.

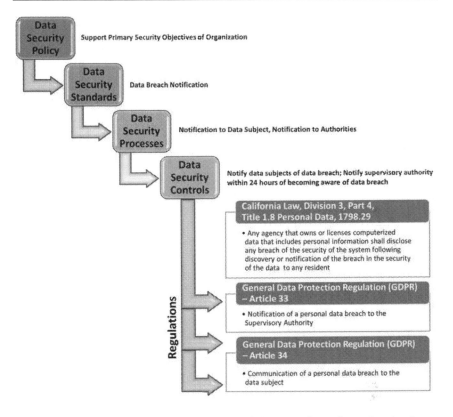

Figure 2.1: The relationship between data security policy, standards, processes, and controls

Policy

A sample policy for the data security management used in Figure 2.1 is as follows:

> Data security is a discipline that is strategic and highly valuable to the organization. The organization must comply with all approved Information Security Standards. The organization has an obligation to its members and business partners to ensure that a governance framework and appropriate measures are in place to protect data and information.

Standards

The data security standards that would apply to this policy are as follows:

- *Confidentiality and Integrity*—The data governance team must maintain accountability for the security and privacy of data within their respective taxonomies.

- *Improper and Unethical Use*—Define and establish data- and information-sharing agreements for internal and external distribution of critical data.

- *Protection from Breaches*—Define business rules for the acceptable use of critical data elements and critical data sets.

Processes

The "Protection from Breaches" standard links to the "Notification to Data Subject" and "Notification to Authorities" processes. These processes state that information executives need a mechanism to enforce the timed communication, or "notification," relating to the data breach. These time-sensitive notifications will govern the communication with data subjects and supervisory authorities.

Controls

With the assistance of an organization's legal and compliance departments, the regulatory controls can be mapped to the standards to ensure adherence to laws, rules, and regulations. Depending on where an organization does business globally, there may be a need to review data protection and privacy laws from a myriad of countries. This mapping can be performed using tools to ensure automation and validate data sovereignty.

Figure 2.2 brings together multiple data governance assets to support data sovereignty compliance with Collibra®. In Canada, two major pieces of legislation govern data sovereignty: the Personal Information Protection and Electronic Documents Act and Canada's Anti-Spam Law. The relevant portions of PIPEDA are Sections 4, 6.1, 7(1), 5(3), and 7(2). The relevant portions of CASL are Sections 6(1), 6(2), and 6(3). The CASL sections govern a control that states, "Email campaigns should be signed off by legal and compliance." This control is also governed by GDPR; essentially, both CASL and GDPR require controllers to have opt-ins before sending out marketing emails. The control governs two critical data elements: "email address" and "do not email." Finally, email address is represented by a column called EMAIL. Collibra is able to tie together all the data governance assets into a single traceability diagram.

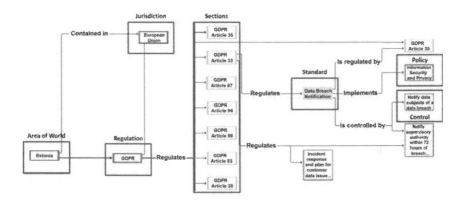

Figure 2.2: Tying jurisdictions, regulations, sections, controls, standards, and policies in Collibra

Summary

The data governance playbook is a key artifact that documents policies, standards, processes, and controls to operationalize data governance. Data policies are guidelines for the appropriate management of an organization's data. Data standards are high-level statements that provide detailed rules about how to implement data policies; they need more detail before they can be operationalized. Data processes provide detailed tasks to implement a standard, including special instructions for the successful implementation of data standards. Data controls are detailed procedures to report regulatory and data governance program adherence. Many regulations can be tied to a single policy, standard, or process. One or more data standards may support each data policy; one or more data processes may support each data standard; and one or more controls may support each data process.

3

Data Taxonomy

Regulation sample	Description
German Federal Data Protection Act, Section 9	Technical and organizational measures— "Public and private bodies processing personal data either on their own behalf or on behalf of others shall take the technical and organizational measures necessary to ensure the implementation of the provisions of this Act. . . ."
European Union General Data Protection Regulation, Article 88(2)	Processing in the context of employment— "Those rules shall include suitable and specific measures to safeguard the data subject's human dignity, legitimate interests, and fundamental rights, with particular regard to the transparency of processing, the transfer of personal data within a group of undertakings, or a group of enterprises engaged in a joint economic activity, and monitoring systems at the work place."
European Union General Data Protection Regulation, Article 9(1)	Processing of special categories of personal data— "Processing of personal data revealing racial or ethnic origin, political opinions, religious or philosophical beliefs, or trade union membership, and the processing of genetic data, biometric data for the purpose of uniquely identifying a natural person, data concerning health, or data concerning a natural person's sex life or sexual orientation shall be prohibited."

A data category is a logical classification of information based on common characteristics of data that is developed by an organization to efficiently use, manage, and protect data and support data governance. Data categories are a requisite to setting acceptable use standards.

Define Level 1 Data Categories in Collaboration with Data Architecture

The data governance and data architecture teams need to collaborate to define the data categories for the enterprise. The initial classification of data categories may be based on an enterprise conceptual model or an enterprise logical data model.

The definition of the level 1 data categories is often a tug-of-war between the data governance, data architecture, legal, and compliance teams. Data architecture may define a data category, but data governance may find it difficult to identify a data owner for that category. In addition, legal and compliance may need a slightly different set of data categories to support the formulation of acceptable use standards.

Define Level 2 and Lower Data Categories

The next step is to define level 2 and lower data categories. As shown in Figure 3.1, customer and employee are level 1 data categories. Customer may be further broken down into contacts, identity, geolocation data, and web and social media. Next, contacts may be further classified as phone, email, address, and preferences. In addition, web and social media may be further classified into Facebook, Twitter®, chat logs, and web cookies. Finally, address yields several level 4 data categories: billing address, mailing address, and seasonal address.

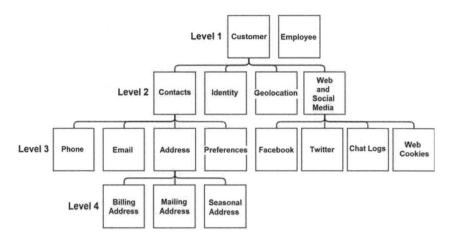

Figure 3.1: Sample hierarchy of data categories to support acceptable use

Figure 3.2 depicts a similar cascading of levels of data categories for employee. In addition to a contacts data category, there are data categories specific to employee information, such as salary and benefits, identity, protected health information, social media, and performance. The image also shows the level 3 data categories for identity: name, gender, date of birth, and national ID. Finally, Facebook, Twitter, and LinkedIn are level 3 categories for social media.

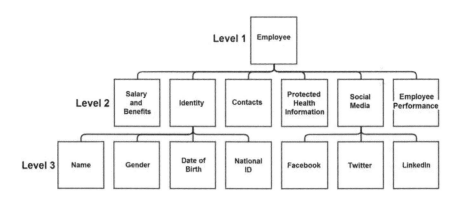

Figure 3.2: Sample hierarchy of employee data categories

Conduct a Sanity Check That Each Data Category Has Clearly Defined Ownership, Especially from a Regulatory Perspective

The German Federal Data Protection Act, Section 9 (Technical and organizational measures) states that public and private bodies processing personal data either on their own behalf or on behalf of others shall take the technical and organizational measures necessary to ensure the implementation of the provisions in the act.

The next step is to ensure that each data category has clearly defined ownership. For example, customer may not be an appropriate level 1 data category for a large multinational financial services organization because there is no owner for customer data across the enterprise. However, as Figure 3.3 demonstrates, customer may be a more appropriate Level 4 data category.

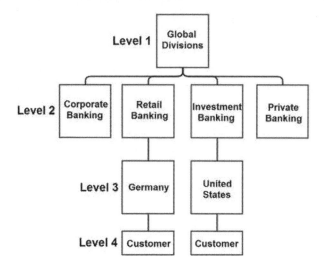

Figure 3.3: Multiple level 4 data categories for customer at a large bank

In this example, a bank needs to assign a specific owner for customer data within retail banking in Germany due to data privacy laws. Similarly, the bank can easily assign an owner for investment banking customer data within the United States. Although customer had no owner at level 1, the legal and organizational framework in which the bank operates day to day may make it the best choice to create multiple level 4 data categories for customer across various divisions and regions. This framework allows the bank to set data collection and acceptable use standards separately by business unit and geography to comply with local business requirements and regulations.

Figure 3.4 shows a simple taxonomy for employee data in Collibra. The level 2 categories under employee include building, identity, others, salary, social media, and HR operations.

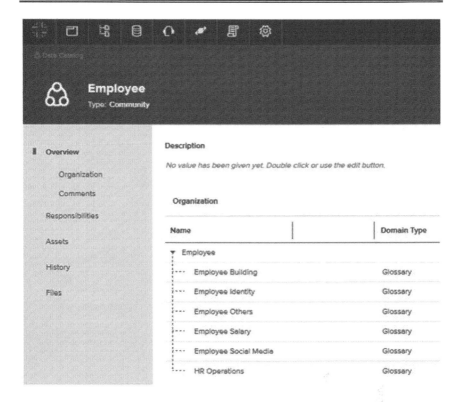

Figure 3.4: Taxonomy depicted in Collibra

Summary

A data category is a logical classification of information to support data governance. Determining the organization's data categorization requires collaboration by architecture, data governance, legal, and compliance. Once the data landscape has been parsed into a framework, ownership can be more easily determined.

4

Data Ownership

Regulation sample	Description
European Union General Data Protection Regulation, Article 37(2)	Designation of the data protection officer— "A group of undertakings may appoint a single data protection officer provided that a data protection officer is easily accessible from each establishment."
European Union General Data Protection Regulation, Article 38(3)	Position of the data protection officer— "The controller and processor shall ensure that the data protection officer does not receive any instructions regarding the exercise of those tasks. He or she shall not be dismissed or penalized by the controller or the processor for performing his tasks. The data protection officer shall directly report to the highest management level of the controller or the processor."
European Union General Data Protection Regulation, Article 47(2)	Binding corporate rules— ". . .the tasks of any data protection officer designated in accordance with Article 37 or any other person or entity in charge of the monitoring compliance with the binding corporate rules within the group of undertakings, or group of enterprises engaged in a joint economic activity, as well as monitoring training and complaint-handling. . ."
Canada Personal Information Protected and Electronic Documents Act, Section 2, Subsection 12(1)	Powers of commissioner— ". . .summon and enforce the appearance of persons before the Commissioner and compel them to give oral or written evidence on oath and to produce any records and things that the Commissioner considers necessary to investigate the complaint, in the same manner and to the same extent as a superior court of record. . ."
Canada Personal Information Protected and Electronic Documents Act, Section 2, Subsection 18(2)	Delegation— "The Commissioner may delegate any of the powers set out in subsection (1)."

Continued

Regulation sample	Description
Singapore Personal Data Protection Act, Section 11(3)	Compliance with act— "An organization shall designate one or more individuals to be responsible for ensuring that the organization complies with this Act."
Australian Privacy Act of 1988, Principle 1.1	Open and transparent management of personal information— "The object of this principle is to ensure that APP entities manage personal information in an open and transparent way."
Australian Privacy Act of 1988, Principle 2.1	Anonymity and pseudonymity— "Individuals must have the option of not identifying themselves, or of using a pseudonym, when dealing with an APP entity in relation to a particular matter."
Irish Data Protection Acts of 1998 and 2003, Section 9(1)	The commissioner— "For the purposes of this Act, there shall be a person (referred to in this Act as the Commissioner) who shall be known as an Coimisinéir Cosanta Sonraí or, in the English language, the Data Protection Commissioner; the Commissioner shall perform the functions conferred on him by this Act."

Data Owners

Data ownership refers to the process of identifying and aligning the individuals within an organization who will be accountable for the trustworthiness and safeguarding of data within their purview. A major component of compliance with data sovereignty regulations is the need to demonstrate, via an individual or designated people, the ability to fully understand regulatory requirements and to ensure that obligations for data processing and data protection are being executed. With today's adoption of cloud computing, multiple points of data processing, access, and transfers, it is critical for an organization to have clear ownership and the appropriate controls in place to drive data ownership.

These controls need to be present at multiple levels:

- Does the organization have the appropriate data governance roles (e.g., data protection officer, executive sponsor, data governance executive)?

- Does the organization have the appropriate data stewardship roles to support data ownership (e.g., data owner, data steward)?

- Does the organization have the appropriate groups to act as decision-making bodies (e.g., enterprise data governance council, regional data governance councils, business-specific data governance councils, data stewardship forums)?

Governance Role: Executive Sponsor

The attesting executive for regulatory and audit reports is generally the executive sponsor for the data governance program. This individual is typically the chief risk officer or the chief financial officer. The executive sponsor holds ultimate accountability for the data governance program. He or she champions data governance with executive staff, facilitates consistent and ongoing support, and holds overall funding for the program.

Governance Role: Data Governance Executive

This data governance executive role is accountable for data governance. The role may be carried out by a company's chief data officer, or, in the case of large organizations, there may be multiple data governance executives representing the company's different business units. Specific responsibilities of the data governance executive (or executives) include the following:

- Form and maintain a data governance framework and required disciplines

- Establish technology and data processing information architecture initiatives to support the regulatory requirements for handling and processing personal data

- Work with data owners, IT, legal, risk, and compliance to educate business areas about how operational changes and activities impact data and information

- Develop a strategic data sovereignty governance roadmap

In a large organization, the data governance executive may appoint data governance leads to drive and manage governance initiatives. These leads would be responsible for appointing the necessary resources, developing governance/data management disciplines, establishing communication channels, and issuing escalation/resolution protocols.

Stewardship Role: Data Owner

The data owner is a senior leader who is ultimately accountable for the trustworthiness and safeguarding of information within his or her respective domain. Taking the example from Chapter 3, the data owner for customer data in the U.S. investment bank may be the chief operating officer for the bank. The data owner is responsible for the following:

- Appoint data stewards who have day-to-day oversight responsibility for the data

- Identify critical data elements for a data domain/category

- Define and manage data standards and own decision rights for data elements (e.g., business definitions, acceptable use, security and privacy requirements, and data quality rules)

- Collaborate and provide input for the approval of data governance standards and processes

- Remediate deficiencies identified through assessments and internal/external audits

Stewardship Role: Data Steward

Each data owner should appoint one or more data stewards to whom the day-to-day responsibilities of data governance and data management can be delegated. Working together with the data owner, the role of the data steward is to ensure that the data governance requirements and controls defined for data elements are in place and maintained on a sustained basis. The responsibilities of the data steward include the following:

- Work with data owners, data protection/compliance partners, and business and IT subject matter experts (SMEs) to translate the requirements of sovereignty regulations to CDE-specific governance standards and processes

- Define and manage business metadata, including common business vocabularies, allowable values, business rules, and data quality rules

- Support information lifecycle management to adhere to retention standards and processes

- Identify, investigate, and resolve data quality issues

- Help data security and privacy offices implement and govern controls to improve adherence to security and privacy policies and standards in place (e.g., validate/revalidate data access, identify sensitive data, define business rules for information ethics, enact data storage and transfer requirements)

- Act as subject matter expert in interactions with peers

Data Sovereignty Role: Data Protection Officer

With respect to meeting the requirements of specific regulations, the appointment of a data protection officer (DPO) can assist in providing an organization with someone with strong knowledge of data protection and sovereignty laws who works with executive governance program sponsors, advising on data processing activities, regulatory compliance, and risk avoidance. The DPO most likely will report to the highest management level within the organization. The responsibilities of the DPO include the following:

- Support the organization's regular and systematic monitoring of data subjects on a large scale, where the core activities consist of processing personal, private, or personally identifiable data

- Inform the organization and its employees who are processing personal data of their obligations under data sovereignty laws

- Monitor compliance with regulations and with the organization's policies related to the protection of personal data

- Become familiar with and monitor adherence to data sovereignty regulations (e.g., the Australian Privacy Act of 1988, Canada's CASL and PIPEDA, the EU's GDPR, Singapore's PDPA)

- Provide advice regarding privacy impact assessments

- Act as a point of contact for and cooperate with supervisory authority/authorities/regulators

- Provide rapid response for any issue regarding the protection of personal data, and report incidents to executive management

- Raise awareness and provide training and education regarding processing, operations, and audits

Legal, Risk, Compliance, and Privacy Professionals

Legal, risk, compliance, and privacy professionals are integral participants in the acceptable use process. These professionals are responsible for the following:

- Provide subject matter expertise on relevant legislation that impacts acceptable use of customer, employee, and other information

- Provide subject matter expertise on best practices in the industry that impact acceptable use of customer, employee, and other information

- Provide input so that the business can make a tradeoff between risk and rewards associated with the use of customer and employee information for analytical and operational use cases

- Sign off on data standards for acceptable use of information

- Provide input and signoff on privacy impact assessments

- Sign off on the format of data sharing agreements

Figures 4.1 and 4.2 depict sample data governance and stewardship organizational models.

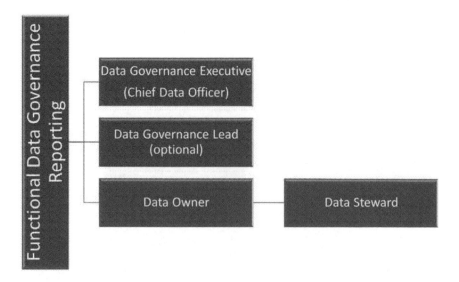

Figure 4.1: Functional reporting with stewardship roles reporting up to the governance roles

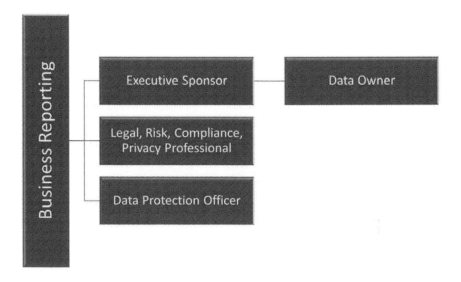

Figure 4.2: Business reporting depicting the relationship of the business's data sovereignty, governance, and stewardship role interaction

The data sovereignty team can manage an inventory of regulations in Collibra. In Figure 4.3, Canada's Anti-Spam Legislation (CASL) is a data sovereignty regulation that applies to Canada.

Figure 4.3: Inventory of regulations in Collibra for easy management and application

Groups: Enterprise Data Governance Council

The data governance executive should establish an overall decision-making body at the enterprise level to set the overall direction of governance in alignment with core business strategies and regulatory requirements. The responsibilities of the enterprise data governance council include the following:

- Champion the strategy and roadmap for enterprise data governance

- Set direction and objectives

- Align governance needs with data protection programs and regulatory requirements

- Approve the data governance policies, standards, and processes

- Approve funding for data governance projects, including consulting and tools

- Review progress against data governance milestones

- Approve the appointment of data owners

- Manage escalated conflicts, as appropriate

Groups: Region- and Business-Specific Data Governance Councils

Any large, multinational financial services institution will probably need region- and/or business-specific data governance councils to address local needs. For example, a multinational financial institution such as the one modeled in Chapter 3 (Figure 3.3) may have a global data governance council in addition to business-specific councils within corporate banking, retail banking, risk, and treasury. The organization may also need data governance councils or advisory groups in specific countries to address the needs of jurisdictional regulations. The responsibilities of such councils include the following:

- Operationalize governance strategy and objectives

- Ensure adoption and lead compliance requirements

- Establish accountability and ownership of data governance and information management

Groups: Forums for Data Stewards

A proposed best practice is the establishment of working governance forums where data stewards can collaborate with business and technical SMEs to manage data requirements and resolve issues at their level without bringing matters to the data governance council. Activities at these forums include the following:

- Share information about data governance best practices relating to metadata, reference data, and data quality

- Resolve conflicts before they need to be brought to the data governance council

- Monitor and triage the resolution of data issues, identifying and collaborating with the necessary business and/or IT subject matter experts

Figure 4.4 describes a sample organizational model for data governance groups.

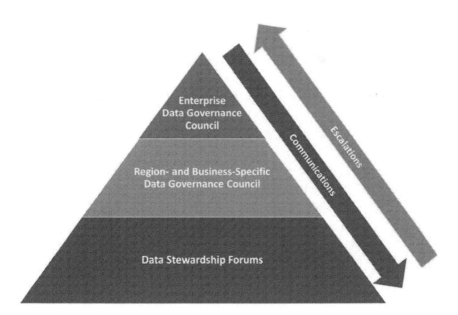

Figure 4.4: Data governance groups

Summary

Data ownership is the process of identifying individuals who will be accountable for the trustworthiness and safeguarding of data within their purview. It is a key control to support compliance with data sovereignty laws. Data governance roles, such as executive sponsor, data governance executive, and potentially data governance leads, as well as data stewardship roles, such as data owners, and data stewards, facilitate the concept of data ownership. In addition, specific data sovereignty regulations may require the need for a data protection officer. It is critical to establish strong collaboration among these roles, business and IT SMEs, and legal, risk, and compliance departments to be successful in data sovereignty compliance.

5

Critical Data Sets and Critical Data Elements

Regulation sample	Description
European Union General Data Protection Regulation, Article 87	Processing of the national identification number— "Member States may further determine the specific conditions for the processing of a national identification number or any other identifier of general application. In that case the national identification number or any other identifier of general application shall be used only under appropriate safeguards for the rights and freedoms of the data subject pursuant to this Regulation."
European Union General Data Protection Regulation, Article 88(1)	Processing in the context of employment— "Member States may, by law or by collective agreements, provide for more specific rules to ensure the protection of the rights and freedoms in respect of the processing of employees' personal data in the employment context, in particular for the purposes of the recruitment, the performance of the contract of employment, including discharge of obligations laid down by law or by collective agreements, management, planning and organization of work, equality and diversity in the workplace, health and safety at work, protection of employer's or customer's property, and for the purposes of the exercise and enjoyment, on an individual or collective basis, of rights and benefits related to employment, and for the purpose of the termination of the employment relationship."
Singapore Personal Data Protection Act, Section 24	Protection of personal data— "An organization shall protect personal data in its possession or under its control by making reasonable security arrangements to prevent unauthorized access, collection, use, disclosure, copying, modification, disposal, or similar risks."

Continued

Regulation sample	Description
South Korea Personal Information Protection Act, Article 24(1)	Limitation to processing unique identifier— "The personal information processor shall not, except the cases stated in the following subparagraphs, process the identifier assigned so as to identify an individual in accordance with laws and regulations, as stated by the Presidential Decree (hereinafter referred to as the 'Unique Identifier'). . . ."

Identify Critical Data Sets

In the context of data sovereignty, critical data sets are groupings or collections of data that may cause operational, regulatory, or financial risk if they are not collected or if they are incorrect, compromised, or used inappropriately.

Critical Data Elements

In the context of data sovereignty, critical data elements are data elements that may cause significant operational, regulatory, or financial risk if they are not collected or if they are incorrect, compromised, or used inappropriately. CDEs may be base attributes (such as customer name) or derived terms (such as high-value customer). The rule of thumb is that CDEs should generally constitute not more than 5 to 10 percent of the total number of attributes under consideration.

Data sovereignty regulations will have a significant impact on CDE identification. Critical data sets may contain CDEs. For example, Facebook data is a critical data set, while Facebook ID is a critical data element. Depending on business requirements and regulations, data standards are best set either for a data set or for a CDE.

Define Template for Critical Data Elements

To capture metadata relating to CDEs, the data governance team needs to provide data stewards with a template such as the one shown in Table 5.1.

Table 5.1: Template for critical data set or critical data element	
Attribute	**Description**
Name	Name of business term that is classified as a critical data set or CDE
Level 1 data category	Name of level 1 data category in the information hierarchy (e.g., Employee)
Level 2 data category	Name of level 2 data category in the information hierarchy, if applicable
Level 3 data category	Name of level 3 data category in the information hierarchy, if applicable
Level 4 data category	Name of level 4 data category in the information hierarchy, if applicable
Definition	Meaning of the business term within the business context
Definition source	Source that provides the definition for the business term
Acronym	Shorthand formed from initial letters of term (e.g., DOB for Date of Birth)
Calculation	Algorithm used to produce a business term
Authoritative data source	Approved repository for a given business term, data element, or attribute
Synonyms	Relation between business terms with the same definition (e.g., vendor and supplier)
Is a type of/has types	Relation to show that a business term is a type of another
Related terms	Relation to link business terms that are not synonyms or types
Reference data	Defined set of values for a business term (e.g., U.S. state codes)
Information security classification	Classification for information security purposes (e.g., public, internal, confidential, highly confidential, secret, restricted)
Controls	Controls that govern the business term (e.g., the Do Not Collect control governs the business term "Race")
Regulations	Regulations that govern the business term (e.g., CASL governs email address)
Data consumers	Business terms, reports, models, systems, and other artifacts that consume the CDE
Data producers	Business terms, models, systems, columns, fields, and other artifacts that produce the CDE
Data quality rules	Rules to define data quality classified by data quality dimension
Data owner	Name of individual who is ultimately accountable for the data
Data owner title	Title of individual who is ultimately accountable for the data
Data steward	Name of individual who works with data on a day-to-day basis
Data steward title	Title of individual who works with data on a day-to-day basis

Populate Template for Critical Data Sets and Critical Data Elements

Once the templates are provided, the data stewards need to populate the template for each CDE or critical data set. Table 5.2 shows a sample populated template using the Patient Account Number CDE. Table 5.3 shows a sample populated template using the Web Cookies data set.

Figure 5.1 shows a list of critical data elements for employee identity information in Collibra. These CDEs include date of birth, employee, employee ID, previous employers, primary mailing address, and Social Security number.

Table 5.2: CDE template for Patient Account Number	
Attribute	**Description**
Name	Patient Account Number
Level 1 data category	Patient
Level 2 data category	Identity
Level 3 data category	Account Number
Level 4 data category	Not applicable
Definition	This number is unique and is assigned to only one patient. It can be used to obtain electronic medical record data as well as patient payment history and medical claims data.
Authoritative data source	Customer Master Data Management Hub
Reports that consume this data	U.S. Department of Health and Human Services quarterly report, U.S. Health Insurance Portability and Accountability Act (HIPAA) reports, federal and state communicable disease reports
Information security classification	Protected
Data consumers	WebMD®, primary operational processing system, payment processing system, customer database
Data producers	Customer database
Related terms	Pt_Acct_Num
Data owner	Jane Wells
Data owner title	Vice President, Medical Policy
Data steward	Jack Smith
Data steward title	Medical Policy Data Manager

Table 5.3: Critical data set template for Web Cookies	
Data set	Description
Name	Web Cookies
Definition	A web cookie is a small piece of data that a website asks the browser to store on the computer or mobile device. The cookie allows the website to "remember" a user's actions or preferences over time.[1]
Information security classification	Internal: When cookie IDs are not combined with any other customer information. Confidential: When cookie IDs are combined with other customer information.
Controls	Obtain user consent before placing web cookies on user devices.
Regulation	Article 5(3) of the European Union ePrivacy Directive requires prior informed consent for storage of or access to information stored on a user's terminal equipment. In other words, websites must ask users whether they agree to most cookies and similar technologies, such as web beacons and flash cookies, before the site starts to use them.[2]

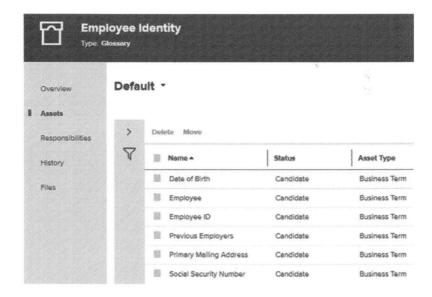

Figure 5.1: Sample of critical data elements associated with an employee in Collibra

---

[1] European Commission, Information Providers Guide, The EU Internet Handbook, "Cookies," http://ec.europa.eu/ipg/basics/legal/cookies/index_en.htm.
[2] Ibid.

Summary

Critical data elements are the 5 to 10 percent of data elements that are determined to be vital to the success of an organization; they represent significant data sovereignty risk. Data sovereignty regulations will have a significant impact on critical data set and critical data element identification. Data governance teams should establish a template to gather metadata for critical data sets and CDEs.

6

Data Collection
and Acceptable Use Standards

Regulation sample	Description
Australian Privacy Act of 1988, Principle 3.1	Collection of solicited personal information— "If an APP entity is an agency, the entity must not collect personal information (other than sensitive information) unless the information is reasonably necessary for, or directly related to, one or more of the entity's functions or activities."
Australian Privacy Act of 1988, Principle 11.1	Security of personal information— "If an APP entity holds personal information, the entity must take such steps as are reasonable in the circumstances to protect the information: (a) from misuse, interference, and loss; and (b) from unauthorized access, modification, or disclosure. . . ."
Russian Federal Law 152-FZ, Chapter 2, Article 6	The processing of personal data— ". . .the operator may entrust the processing of personal data to another person with the consent of the subject of personal data, unless otherwise stipulated in the Federal law, on the basis of a concluded contract with that person. . . ."
European Union General Data Protection Regulation, Article 6(1)	Lawfulness of processing— "Processing shall be lawful only if and to the extent that at least one of the following applies. . . ."
European Union General Data Protection Regulation, Article 7(1)	Conditions for consent— "Where processing is based on consent, the controller shall be able to demonstrate that the data subject has consented to processing of his or her personal data. . . ."

Continued

Regulation sample	Description
European Union General Data Protection Regulation, Article 30(1)	Records of processing activities— "Each controller. . .shall maintain a record of processing activities under its responsibility. That record shall contain all of the following information: (a) the name and contact details of the controller and, where applicable, the joint controller, the controller's representative, and the data protection officer; (b) the purposes of the processing; (c) a description of the categories of data subjects and of the categories of personal data; (d) the categories of recipients to whom the personal data have been or will be disclosed including recipients in third countries or international organizations; (e) where applicable, transfers of personal data to a third country or an international organization. . . ."
Irish Data Protection Acts of 1998 and 2003, Section 2	Collection, processing, keeping, use, and disclosure of personal data— ". . .the data— (i) shall have been obtained only for one or more specified, explicit, and legitimate purposes, (ii) shall not be further processed in a manner incompatible with that purpose or those purposes, (iii) shall be adequate, relevant, and not excessive in relation to the purpose or purposes for which they were collected or are further processed, and (iv) shall not be kept for longer than is necessary for that purpose or those purposes. . ."
Canada Personal Information Protected and Electronic Documents, Section 1, Subsection 7(1) and 7(2)	Collection without knowledge or consent— ". . .an organization may collect personal information without the knowledge or consent of the individual only if. . . ." Use without knowledge or consent— ". . .an organization may, without the knowledge or consent of the individual, use personal information only if. . . ."
Singapore Personal Data Protection Act, Second Schedule	Collection of personal data without consent— "An organization may collect personal data about an individual without the consent of the individual or from a source other than the individual in any of the following circumstances. . . ."

California Civil Code Section 1747–1748.7, Title 1.3 Credit Cards, Section 1747	Song-Beverly Credit Card Act of 1971— ". . .no person, firm, partnership, association, or corporation which accepts credit cards for the transaction of business shall do any of the following: . . .Request. . .the cardholder to provide personal identification information. . . ."

Data sovereignty regulations often require organizations to conform to data collection and acceptable use standards.

Minimize Data Collection

GDPR Article 5(1)(c) states that personal data shall be adequate, relevant, and limited to what is necessary in relation to the purposes for which they are processed ("data minimization"). In other words, controllers should not collect personal data that is in excess of what is legitimately required for processing purposes.

Case Study 6.1: California Supreme Court rules that retailers collecting ZIP codes violate a customer's privacy rights[1]

In February 2011, the California Supreme Court ruled against the housewares retailer Williams-Sonoma in a class action lawsuit. The court ruled that retail stores could not ask a customer to provide a U.S. postal ZIP code in the course of a credit card transaction. The plaintiff alleged that Williams-Sonoma used customer ZIP codes to obtain customer home addresses and then used the data for marketing or sold the information to other businesses. The plaintiff claimed that the practice breached her right to privacy under the California Constitution and violated the Song-Beverly Credit Card Act of 1971.

Figure 6.1 shows a prohibited customer data collection standard in IBM® InfoSphere® Information Governance Catalog (IGC). The data standard states that processing of personal data revealing racial or ethnic origin, political opinions, religious or philosophical beliefs, trade-union membership, and the processing of genetic data are prohibited unless approved by the legal department. This data standard implements an overall customer data governance policy and is associated with GDPR Article 9.

---

[1] Terry Baynes, "California Court Rules Against Williams-Sonoma," Reuters (February 10, 2011), http://www.reuters.com/article/2011/02/11/us-williamssonoma-idUSTRE71A0BW20110211.

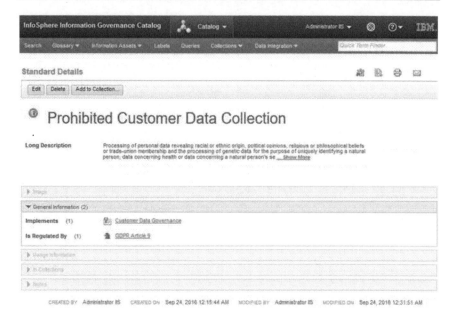

*Figure 6.1: IBM InfoSphere Information Governance Catalog supporting
data collection standards—prohibited customer data collection*

Obtain Consent from Minors

Per GDPR Article 8 (Conditions applicable to child's consent in relation
to information society services), an organization must be able to demonstrate that a data subject has consented to processing of his or her personal
data. Table 6.1 reviews informed consent pertaining to minors in the European Union.

Obtain Informed Consent

Article 7(1) of the GDPR states that where processing is based on
consent, the controller shall be able to demonstrate that the data subject
has consented to processing of his or her personal data. Table 6.2 reviews
informed consent pertaining to clinical trials in the United States and the
European Union, with the latter appearing to be more restrictive.

Table 6.1: Consent by minors	
Data set	Personal data, potentially including IP addresses and mobile device IDs
Data subject	Minors
Regulations and restrictions	European Union GDPR Article 8— A child, age 16 and over, is lawfully permitted to provide consent when their data processing is in question. If the child is below the age of 16, processing of data is lawful only if the parent or legal guardian of the child provides consent. Member states may provide by law for a lower age, provided that such lower age is not below 13 years. United States Children's Online Privacy Protection Act (COPPA)[2]— Parental consent is required for websites that collect personal information for children under the age of 13.

Table 6.2: Consent by patients in clinical trials	
Data set	Clinical trials
Data subject	Patients
Regulations and restrictions	Part 50, Section 50.20 of the U.S. Food and Drug Administration Code of Federal Regulations Title 21— Investigators cannot involve human beings in any research without effective informed consent. The informed consent language must be easy to understand by the data subject to allow for participation consideration without coercion or undue influence. Informed consent is not an attempt to waive a data subject's legal rights or hold harmless an investigator, institution, or organization from negligent liability.[3] European Union GDPR Recital 33— "It is often not possible to fully identify the purpose of personal data processing for scientific research purposes at the time of data collection. Therefore, data subjects should be allowed to give their consent to certain areas of scientific research when in keeping with recognized ethical standards for scientific research. Data subjects should have the opportunity to give their consent only to certain areas of research or parts of research projects to the extent allowed by the intended purpose."

---

[2] U.S. Federal Trade Commission, "Children's Online Privacy Protection Rule ('COPPA')," https://www.ftc.gov/enforcement/rules/rulemaking-regulatory-reform-proceedings/childrens-online-privacy-protection-rule.

[3] U.S. Food and Drug Administration, CFR–Code of Federal Regulations Title 21, http://www.accessdata.fda.gov/scripts/cdrh/cfdocs/cfcfr/CFRSearch.cfm?fr=50.20& SearchTerm=informed%20consent.

Table 6.3 reviews opt-in and opt-out requirements for email marketing campaigns in Canada.

Table 6.3: Opt-in requirements for email marketing campaigns in Canada	
Data set	Marketing preferences (email address, do not email indicator)
Data subject	Any potential recipient of a marketing email
Jurisdiction	Canada
Regulations	CASL Section 6
Restrictions	Recipients need to provide opt-in consent to receive marketing emails.

Figure 6.2 shows a consistent customer data collection standard in IBM InfoSphere Information Governance Catalog. The data standard states that certain customer data categories, such as identity and contact information, may be collected provided the customer has given consent. This data standard implements the overall customer data governance policy and is implemented by a specific control related to the approval of customer data collection.

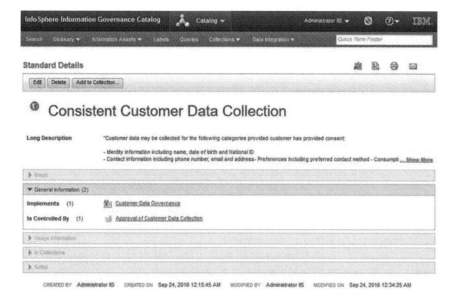

Figure 6.2: IBM InfoSphere Information Governance Catalog supporting data collection standards—consistent customer data collection

Establish Acceptable Use Standards for Critical Data

GDPR Article 6 – Lawfulness of Processing[4]

1. Processing shall be lawful only if and to the extent that at least one of the following applies:

   a. the data subject has given consent to the processing of his or her personal data for one or more specific purposes;

   b. processing is necessary for the performance of a contract to which the data subject is party or in order to take steps at the request of the data subject prior to entering into a contract;

   c. processing is necessary for compliance with a legal obligation to which the controller is subject;

   d. processing is necessary in order to protect the vital interests of the data subject or of another natural person;

   e. processing is necessary for the performance of a task carried out in the public interest or in the exercise of official authority vested in the controller;

   f. processing is necessary for the purposes of the legitimate interests pursued by the controller or by a third party, except where such interests are overridden by the interests or fundamental rights and freedoms of the data subject which require protection of personal data, in particular where the data subject is a child.

As shown in Figure 6.3, the data governance team can use Collibra to manage data standards for critical data elements. The acceptable use standard for Social Security number states that this information cannot be shared internally or externally. If the numbers are to be shared, then business justification needs to be provided to the human resources department. The data governance team has also classified Social Security number as highly confidential information.

---

[4] EU GDPR Article 6, http://www.privacy-regulation.eu/en/6.htm.

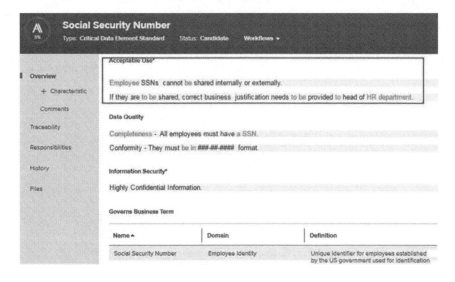

Figure 6.3: Acceptable use of SSN in Collibra

Restrict Secondary Use of the Data

GDPR Article 5 restricts the secondary use of data without consent or other specified reasons. The article states that personal data shall be collected for specified, explicit, and legitimate purposes and not further processed in a manner that is incompatible with those purposes.

A report from the U.S. Federal Trade Commission (FTC) includes the following case study on the potential uses of facial recognition technology in combination with social media[5].

> ### Case Study 6.2: Privacy implications arising from the combination of facial recognition technology and social media
>
> Facial recognition technology enables the identification of an individual based on his or her distinct facial characteristics. While this technology has been used in experiments for more than 30 years, until recently it remained costly and limited under real-world conditions. However, steady improvements in the technology combined with increased computing power have shifted this technology out of the realm of science fiction and into the marketplace.

---

[5] Reproduced from *Protecting Consumer Privacy in an Era of Rapid Change*, U.S. Federal Trade Commission, March 2012, p. 45, https://www.ftc.gov/reports/protecting-consumer-privacy-era-rapid-change-recommendations-businesses-policymakers.

As costs have decreased and accuracy improved, facial recognition software has been incorporated into a variety of commercial products. Today, it can be found in online social networks and photo management software, where it is used to facilitate photo organizing, and in mobile apps, where it is used to enhance gaming. This surge in the deployment of facial recognition technology will likely boost the desire of companies to use data enhancement by offering yet another means to compile and link information about an individual gathered through disparate transactions and contexts.

For instance, social networks such as Facebook and LinkedIn, as well as websites such as Yelp® and Amazon®, all encourage users to upload profile photos and make these photos publicly available. As a result, vast amounts of facial data, often linked with real names and geographic locations, have been made publicly available. A recent paper illustrated how researchers from Carnegie Mellon University were able to combine readily available facial recognition software with data mining algorithms and statistical re-identification techniques to determine, in many cases, an individual's name, location, interests, and even the first five digits of the individual's Social Security number, starting with only the individual's picture.[6]

Companies could easily replicate these results. Today, retailers use facial detection software in digital signs to analyze the age and gender of viewers and deliver targeted advertisements.[7] Facial detection does not uniquely identify an individual. Instead, it detects human faces and determines gender and approximate age range. In the future, digital signs and kiosks placed in supermarkets, transit stations, and college campuses could capture images of viewers and, using facial recognition software, match those faces to online identities and return advertisements based on the websites specific individuals have visited or on the publicly available information contained in their social media profiles.

Retailers could also implement loyalty programs, ask users to associate a photo with their account, and then use the combined data to link the consumers to other online accounts or their in-store actions. This would enable a retailer to glean information about a consumer's purchase habits, interests, and even movements, which it could use to offer discounts on particular products or otherwise market to the consumer.

Continued

[6] Alessandro Acquisti, Ralph Gross, and Fred Stutzman, Face Recognition Study–FAQ, "Faces of Facebook: Privacy in the Age of Augmented Reality," http://www.heinz.cmu.edu/~acquisti/face-recognition-study-FAQ.

[7] Shan Li and David Sarno, "Advertisers Start Using Facial Recognition to Tailor Pitches," *Los Angeles Times* (August 21, 2011), http://articles.latimes.com/2011/aug/21/business/la-fi-facial-recognition-20110821.

The ability of facial recognition technology to identify consumers based solely on a photograph, create linkages between the offline and online world, and compile highly detailed dossiers of information makes it especially important for companies using this technology to implement the appropriate privacy policies.

The FTC report makes a number of recommendations regarding the use of facial data. Organizations should consider these recommendations, although they are not currently legally binding. The recommendations are summarized below:

- Organizations should reduce the amount of time facial information is retained and should adopt reasonable security measures. For example, if a digital sign uses data enhancement to deliver targeted advertisements to viewers, the FTC report suggests that the data should be deleted immediately after the consumer has walked away.

- Organizations should disclose to consumers that the facial data they supply might be used to link them to information from third parties or publicly available sources. For example, if a kiosk is used to invite shoppers to register for a store loyalty program, the shopper should be informed that the photo taken by the kiosk camera and associated with the account might be combined with other data to market discounts and offers to the shopper. Finally, if a company received the data from other sources, it should disclose the sources to the consumer.

Summary

Data sovereignty regulations require organizations to collect only necessary data and to disclose the intended use of the collected data. Organizations need to define standards that explain which uses of data are deemed acceptable; they must be cognizant of all personal data, including for customers, prospects, and employees.

7

Data Security

Regulation sample	Description
Canada Personal Information Protected and Electronic Documents, Provision 4.7, Principle 7	Safeguards— "Personal information shall be protected by security safeguards appropriate to the sensitivity of the information. . . ."
Russian Federal Law 152-FZ, Article 11	Biometric personal data— "Information that characterize the physiological and biological features, based on which you can establish his identity (biometric personal data) and which are used by the operator to establish the identity of the subject of personal data may be processed only with the consent in writing of the subject of personal data, except as provided by part 2 of this article. . . ."
European Union General Data Protection Regulation, Recital 30	Device identifiers— "Natural persons may be associated with online identifiers provided by their devices, applications, tools, and protocols, such as internet protocol addresses, cookie identifiers, or other identifiers such as radio frequency identification tags. This may leave traces which, in particular when combined with unique identifiers and other information received by the servers, may be used to create profiles of the natural persons and identify them."
European Union General Data Protection Regulation, Article 32	Security of processing— ". . .the controller and the processor shall implement appropriate technical and organizational measures to ensure a level of security appropriate to the risk, including inter alia as appropriate: (a) the pseudonymization and encryption of personal data; (b) the ability to ensure the ongoing confidentiality, integrity, availability, and resilience of processing systems and services;. . . ."

Continued

Regulation sample	Description
European Union General Data Protection Regulation, Article 33(1)	Notification of a personal data breach to the supervisory authority— ". . .not later than 72 hours after having become aware of it, notify the personal data breach to the supervisory authority. . . ."
European Union General Data Protection Regulation, Article 34(1)	Communication of a personal data breach to the data subject— "When the personal data breach is likely to result in a high risk to the rights and freedoms of natural persons, the controller shall communicate the personal data breach to the data subject without undue delay. . . ."
Irish Data Protection Acts of 1998 and 2003, Amendment of Section 2 (Biometrics in the Workplace), Section 2C	Security measures for personal data— ". . .(b) ensure that the data processor provides sufficient guarantees in respect of the technical security measures, and organizational measures, governing the processing, and (c) take reasonable steps to ensure compliance with those measures. . . ."
California Civil Code Section 1798	Accounting of disclosures— ". . .The security breach notification shall be written in plain language, shall be titled 'Notice of Data Breach,. . . ."
The 190th General Court of the Commonwealth of Massachusetts, Part 1, Title XV, Chapter 93H, Section 3(a)	Duty to report known security breach or unauthorized use of personal information— "A person or agency that maintains or stores, but does not own or license data that includes personal information about a resident of the commonwealth, shall provide notice, as soon as practicable and without unreasonable delay,. . . ."

Article 32 of the GDPR deals with the security of processing. Taking into account the state of the art, the costs of implementation, and the nature, scope, context, and purposes of processing as well as the risk of varying likelihood and severity for the rights and freedoms of natural persons, the controller and the processor shall implement appropriate technical and organizational measures to ensure a level of security appropriate to the risk.

Before proceeding any further, here is some background on key concepts that will be discussed in this chapter:

Term	Definition
Data anonymization	The process of removing, scrubbing, and redacting personally identifiable information from data sets in an effort to keep a data subject from being identified.
Data masking	The process of systematically transforming sensitive information into realistic, but fictionalized, values.[1]

---

[1] Sunil Soares, *The IBM Data Governance Unified Process* (MC Press, 2010).

Data encryption	The process of rendering sensitive data unreadable so that an attacker cannot gain unauthorized access to it.
Data tokenization	The process of substituting a sensitive data element with a non-sensitive equivalent, referred to as a token, that has no extrinsic or exploitable meaning or value. The token is a reference that maps back to the sensitive data through a tokenization system. The mapping from original data to a token uses methods that render tokens infeasible to reverse in the absence of the tokenization system; for example, using tokens created from random numbers.[2]
Database monitoring	A form of security technology that monitors the activities of the database but operates independently of the database itself. Database monitoring technologies typically have a limited impact on the performance of the database system because they do not monitor database logs.

Establish Controls for Data Security Breach Notification

Many countries are enacting data breach notification requirements (e.g., Canada's Digital Privacy Act (DPA), Senate Bill S-4, which amends PIPEDA; GDPR Articles 33 and 34). Furthermore, as data sovereignty legislation continues to evolve and put further restrictions in place to disallow personal data being transferred outside the country where the data subject resides (e.g., People's Republic of China's Cybersecurity Law, Russian Federal Law 152-FZ), and as companies engage in managing and processing data in a cloud environment, the need to establish controls to deal with possible breaches of data is paramount.

Breach notification laws are established in many U.S. states, and they may differ among states. For example, California Civil Code Section 1798.29(a) requires a business or state agency to notify any California resident whose unencrypted personal information was acquired, or is reasonably believed to have been acquired, by an unauthorized person. Any person or business that is required to issue a security breach notification to more than 500 California residents, as a result of a single breach of the security system, shall electronically submit a single sample copy of that security breach notification, excluding any personally identifiable information, to the state attorney general according to California Civil Code Section 1798.

In the Commonwealth of Massachusetts in the United States, if an individual or organization that produces or consumes data that includes

---

[2] Wikipedia, "Tokenization (data security)," https://en.wikipedia.org/wiki/Tokenization_(data_security).

personal information about a resident of the Commonwealth becomes aware of a data breach, they must send notification as soon as practicable. Data breaches in Massachusetts must be reported to the attorney general, to the director of consumer affairs and business regulation, and to the resident. The notice must include the nature of the breach, the number of residents affected at the time of notification, and any steps toward mitigation that occurred.[3]

Companies need to establish controls to determine when a breach has occurred, implement any remediation plans, and notify data subjects as well as the regulatory authorities, as appropriate.

Define Sensitive Data

Data governance teams must work with legal, privacy, compliance, and the business to define sensitive data. The definition of sensitive data may vary by jurisdiction. Figure 7.1 shows several built-in tags in Waterline Data®. These out-of-the-box tags enable the automated discovery of personal data such as email, IP address, and people names.

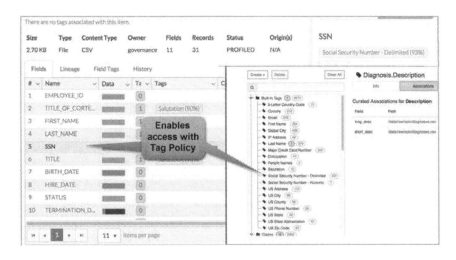

Figure 7.1: Waterline Data's built-in tags for sensitive data types

---

[3] 190th General Court of the Commonwealth of Massachusetts, Part 1, Title XV, Chapter 93H, Section 3.

Establish Data Anonymization Standards

Recital 26 of the GDPR states that the principles of data protection should apply to any information concerning an identified or identifiable natural person. The principles of data protection should therefore not apply to anonymous information, namely information that does not relate to an identified or identifiable natural person, or to personal data rendered anonymous in such a manner that the data subject is not, or is no longer, identifiable.

The data governance office must establish controls to appropriately mask, encrypt, or tokenize sensitive personal data. The data masking standards need to ensure that data cannot be reconstructed when multiple fields are combined.

For example, data scientists may request that the employee name field be masked prior to any analytics. However, a smart data scientist may likely be able to discern the identity of an employee by looking at title, compensation, and gender (e.g., "Director of HR who is a female with base salary of $200,000"). In such situations, it may be more appropriate to also mask job title and to provide a salary band, such as "above $100,000."

Discover Hidden Sensitive Data in Production and Non-Production Environments

The data governance office needs to discover hidden sensitive data in production and non-production environments, and in structured, semi-structured, and unstructured formats. As shown in Figure 7.2, Waterline Data discovers all instances of files that contain sensitive data based on the predefined tags.

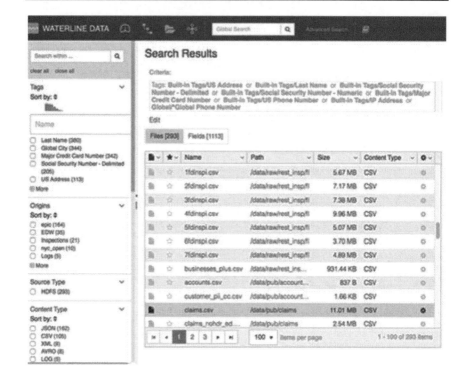

Figure 7.2: Discovery of files containing sensitive data types based on built-in tags in Waterline Data

Anonymize Sensitive Data in Production and Non-Production Environments

The next step is to actually anonymize the data using masking, encryption, or other techniques. As shown in Figure 7.3, Waterline Data also supports data masking for sensitive data that has been discovered based on tags.

In Figure 7.4, IBM DB2®, MySQL™, Oracle®, SAP® Sybase®, and other databases contain sensitive data such as Social Security numbers. If an outsourced database administrator or unauthorized user issues an SQL command against the database, he or she will be able to view only the last four digits of the Social Security number. This is accomplished by dynamic data masking with IBM InfoSphere Guardium®.

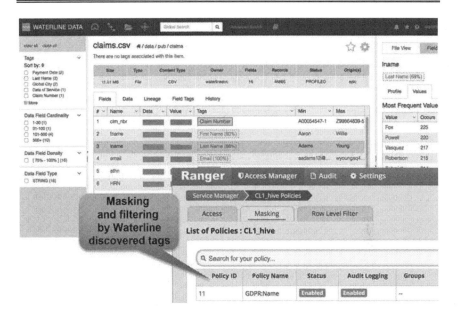

Figure 7.3: Masking of sensitive data that has been discovered
based on Waterline Data's built-in tags

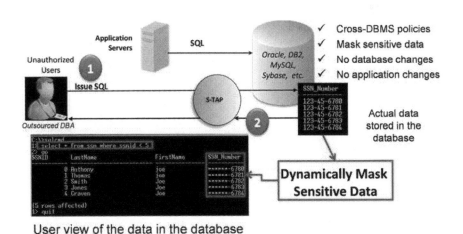

User view of the data in the database

Figure 7.4: Masking Social Security numbers in production databases
in IBM InfoSphere Guardium

Data masking tools also need to mask sensitive data in non-production environments. Tools in this space include IBM InfoSphere Optim™ Data Masking Solution and Informatica® Data Masking solutions. In Figure 7.5, the customer contact database is a non-production application. The contact database contains an Office Phone field that holds sensitive data.

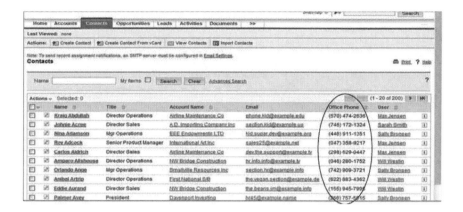

Figure 7.5: Customer contact database containing office phone numbers that are considered sensitive data

In Figure 7.6, IBM InfoSphere Optim Data Masking Solution masks the data in the Office Phone field.

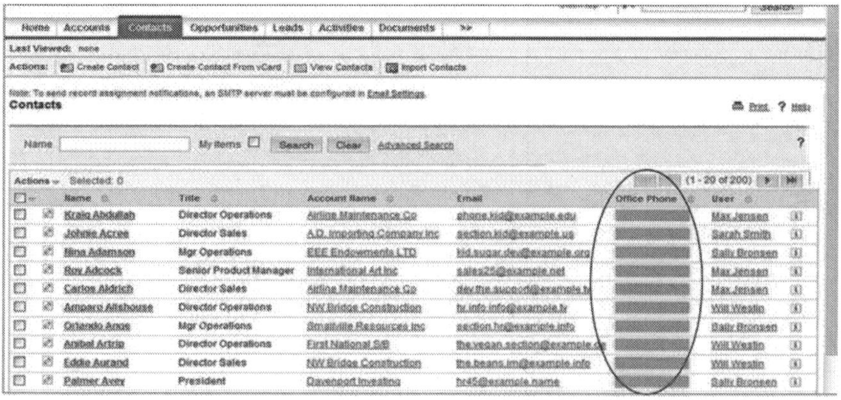

Figure 7.6: Masking office phone numbers in IBM InfoSphere Optim Data Masking Solution

Flag Sensitive Data in the Metadata Repository

Once the data governance team has identified sensitive data, it needs to flag all such instances in the metadata repository. In Figure 7.7, the data steward has flagged the business term "Social Security Number" as sensitive data by setting the custom attribute called "Sensitive Data" to true.

Figure 7.7: Social Security number flagged as sensitive data in Collibra Data Governance Center

Summary

To comply with data sovereignty regulations, organizations must implement the appropriate technological and organizational measures to secure personal information. The data governance team, in conjunction with legal, compliance, technology, and the business, must define "sensitive data," create standards for anonymization, develop discovery procedures, and implement a process to flag that data in the metadata repository.

8

Data Risk Assessments

Regulation sample	Description
Canada's Anti-Spam Law, Provision 10(4)	Express consent, sections 6 to 8— "In addition to the requirements set out in subsections (1) and (3), if the computer program that is to be installed performs one or more of the functions described in subsection (5), the person who seeks express consent must, when requesting consent, clearly and prominently, and separately and apart from the license agreement. . . ."
European Union General Data Protection Regulation, Article 35(1)	Data protection impact assessment— "Where a type of processing in particular using new technologies, and taking into account the nature, scope, context, and purposes of the processing, is likely to result in a high risk to the rights and freedoms of natural persons. . . ."
Irish Data Protection Acts of 1998 and 2003, Amendment of Section 2 (Biometrics in the Workplace), Section 2C	Security measures for personal data— ". . .may have regard to the state of technological development and the cost of implementing the measures, and (b) shall ensure that the measures provide a level of security appropriate. . . ."

Several data sovereignty laws, such as the GDPR and the Irish Data Protection Acts of 1998 and 2003, have instituted formal requirements for data protection impact assessments. According to Article 35 of the GDPR, a data protection impact assessment is an assessment of the impact of processing operations on the protection of personal data.

The GDPR states that the controller shall carry out a data protection impact assessment when a type of processing uses new technologies or is likely to result in a high risk to the rights and freedoms of natural persons. Privacy impact assessment is a term that is often used synonymously with data protection impact assessment.

Develop Template for Data Protection Impact Assessments

Table 8.1 presents a sample template for a data protection impact assessment.

Table 8.1: Data protection impact assessment template	
Impacted systems or processes	List specific systems, databases, applications, or processes that are impacted (e.g., web portal for customer complaints, customer ordering).
Types of data	Identify data sets or data attributes that will be collected or used by the systems, databases, applications, or processes.
Data classification	Explain whether the data is private, protected, or for general use.
How system will use data	Explain the proposed usage of data within the system.
Is data necessary for function (Yes/No)?	Is the data required for proper functioning of the system or process?
Justification of necessity	Provide the business or technical justification for collecting and usage of data.
Data sovereignty laws	Identify any data sovereignty or other privacy laws that may impact this situation.
Data risks	Explain any data risks associated with this system or process (e.g., data breach).
Risk mitigation plan	Describe, at a high-level, a mitigation plan for planned risks (e.g., use sensitive flags, encrypt or mask).

Conduct Data Protection Impact Assessments for High-Risk Data Types

The Irish Data Protection Commissioner has recommended that a documented privacy impact assessment be carried out prior to installing a biometric system in the workplace. Some of the points that might be included in the privacy impact assessment include the following:[1]

- Do I have a time management and/or access control system in place? Why do I feel I need to replace it? What problems are there with the system?

---

[1] Data Protection Commissioner of Ireland, "Biometrics in the workplace," http://dataprotection.ie/viewdoc.asp?DocID=244.

- What are the objectives of the biometric system? Is it for time management purposes and/or for access control purposes? Will non-biometric systems perform the required tasks adequately?

- Do I need a system that identifies employees, as opposed to a verification system?

- Do I need a central database? If so, what is wrong with a system that does not use a central database?

- How accurate should the data be? What procedures are used to ensure accuracy of data? Will the data require updating?

- How will the information be secured? Who will have access to the data or to logs? Why, when, and how will such access be permitted?

- What legal basis do I have for requiring employees to participate?

- Does the system employ additional identifiers (e.g., PIN number, smart card) along with the biometric? If so, would these additional identifiers be sufficient on their own, rather than requiring operation in conjunction with a biometric?

- How will I inform employees about the system? What information about the system do I need to provide to employees?

- Would I be happy if I were an employee asked to use such a system?

- If the introduction of a biometric system is justified, can I offer an alternative system to individuals who may object to the invasion of privacy involved in a biometric system?

- What is my retention policy on biometric data? Can I justify the retention period in my retention policy? Do I have a comprehensive data retention policy? Have I updated this policy to take into account the introduction of a biometric system for staff?

The Commonwealth of Massachusetts provides guidelines for information security risk assessments.[2] The methodology is based on the published methodology developed by the Centers for Medicare and

---

[2] Commonwealth of Massachusetts, "Information Security Risk Assessment Guidelines," http://www.mass.gov/anf/research-and-tech/cyber-security/security-for-state-employees/risk-assessment/risk-assessment-guideline.html.

Medicaid Services (CMS).[3] The HIPAA security framework also calls for due diligence for systems handling electronic protected health information (EPHI); creating an Information Risk Assessment Report from the CMS risk assessment satisfies the HIPAA rule's requirements to analyze risks, formulate appropriate safeguards, and document the risk management decision-making process,[4] and it informs the organization's actions in complying with other parts of the rule.

Smart meter privacy is another area of concern. Case study 8.1 reviews meter privacy considerations in the European Union. Case study 8.2 discusses the privacy framework for smart meters in California.

Case Study 8.1: Smart meter privacy in the European Union[5]

The European Union Article 29 Data Protection Working Party issued opinion 12/2011 on smart metering; the opinion was adopted on April 4, 2011. Some of the key provisions of this opinion include:

- *Personal data*—Due to the presence of a unique identifier that is tied to a specific property, smart meter readings are considered personal data under the European Data Protection Directive 95/46/EC. Privacy is particularly important because detailed smart meter readings can be used to profile the energy consumption and household patterns of customers.

- *Possible grounds for processing of personal data*—Utilities must meet one or more of five possible grounds for the processing of personal data related to smart meters:

  - *Consent*—The customer has made a fully informed decision that is granular enough to reflect different functionalities.

  - *Contract*—Processing of personal data is required to produce a bill based on the smart meter data; however, the contract must provide information about the frequency of meter readings.

---

[3] Centers for Medicare and Medicaid Services (CMS), U.S. Department of Health and Human Services, *CMS Information Security Risk Assessment (IS RA) Procedure,* https://www.cms.gov/Research-Statistics-Data-and-Systems/CMS-Information-Technology/InformationSecurity/downloads/IS_RA_Procedure.pdf.

[4] U.S. Department of Health and Human Services, HIPAA security rule, 45 CFR part 164.308 (a)(1)(ii)(A)(B), https://www.gpo.gov/fdsys/pkg/CFR-2007-title45-vol1/pdf/CFR-2007-title45-vol1-sec164-308.pdf.

[5] This section includes content from *Opinion 12/2011 on Smart Metering,* Article 29 Data Protection Working Party, http://ec.europa.eu/justice/data-protection/article-29/documentation/opinion-recommendation/files/2011/wp183_en.pdf.

o *Public interest or official authority*—The operator is responsible for the performance of the physical network and for reducing electricity consumption.

o *Legal obligation*—The operator has a legal obligation to install smart meters and collect data for every installation.

o *Legitimate interests*—The utility should not use data that is inherently or disproportionately intrusive, such as by creating detailed customer profiles or passing data to third parties without customer knowledge and consent.

- *Privacy by design*—Smart meter implementations should have privacy built in at the start, not just in terms of security measures but also in terms of minimizing the amount of personal data processed. The Working Party states that any data should remain within the household network unless transmission is necessary or if the customer consents to the transmission. The opinion highlights a utility that collects realtime data every 10 to 60 minutes to create load graphs. The load graph is stored inside the meter, with a two-month history, and is collected by the utility only when needed. Finally, the Working Party recommends privacy impact assessments regarding the use of smart meters.

- *Retention of personal data*—The Working Party states that smart meter data should be retained only for as long as necessary. For example, utilities might make smart meter readings available to customers so that they can improve their energy efficiency. In this case, the Working Party states that a retention period of 13 months might be suitable to provide year-on-year comparisons, provided the customer has agreed to take advantage of this functionality. However, a shorter retention period would be appropriate for other services. In many instances, it is conceivable that customers could hold much of the data on the smart meter itself.

- *Crime prevention and investigation*—Smart meter data can also be used to identify suspicious activities, such as indoor marijuana growers using large amounts of electricity. The Working Party states that the mere fact that such a possibility exists does not automatically legitimize wide-scale processing of data to identify potential wrongdoers.

Case Study 8.2: Smart meter privacy in California

The California Public Utility Commission (PUC) has issued decision 11-07-056 adopting rules to protect the privacy and security of the electricity usage data of utility customers. San Diego Gas & Electric® (SDG&E®) and the Information and Privacy Commissioner of Ontario, Canada, released a white paper detailing the best practices to apply privacy by design to the smart meter pricing program at SDG&E.[6]

SDG&E has a chief customer privacy officer as well as a working group that oversees privacy compliance. The chief customer privacy officer is also the vice president of customer services and serves as a member of the executive management team. The chief customer privacy officer is responsible for the completion of privacy impact assessments.

A key feature of SDG&E's privacy by design program is "privacy by default." Said differently, SDG&E's policy is that no action is required by customers who need to opt-in rather than opt-out of default privacy settings.

Conduct Data Protection Impact Assessments for High-Risk Projects

Table 8.2 shows the items that should be included in a comprehensive data protection impact assessment.

Tools such as OneTrust® may be used to collect survey information from large numbers of respondents who may be distributed across multiple business units and geographies. Figure 8.1 shows a simple CASL survey that has been circulated to respondents. The survey includes several questions:

- Do you send out email marketing campaigns?

- Are you complying with "opt-in preferences"?

- Is there a named sender?

- Is there a mechanism to contact the sender?

- Do the emails provide the ability for the recipient to unsubscribe?

- Do the contacts have a validity date?

---

[6] San Diego Gas & Electric and the Information and Privacy Commissioner, Ontario, Canada, *Applying Privacy by Design Best Practices to SDG&E's Smart Pricing Program*, March 2012, https://www.sdge.com/sites/default/files/documents/pbd-sdge_0.pdf.

Table 8.2: Sample data protection impact assessment			
Name of impacted system	Modeling tool 'XYZ'	Data warehouse 'VRB'	Customer portal 'We See You'
How will system use data?	Physical model for customer and employee data	Store customer claim information	Expose customer data
Is data necessary for function?	Yes	Yes	Yes
Justification of necessity	'XYZ' will store all customer and employee data attributes by version	'VRB' data warehouse must capture all information sent by providers on claims	Regulations require that customers view and review data stored by company
Data subject risks identified	Private, protected, sensitive data will be captured, stored, and exposed	Private, protected, sensitive data will be captured, stored, and exposed	Private, protected, sensitive data will be exposed
Risk mitigation plan	When reviewing technical functionality, ensure the use of sensitive flags, encrypt or mask sensitive data where possible	During the functional and technical design phase, ensure that requirements are in place to use sensitive flags, encrypt data and mask as appropriate	During the functional design phase, ensure that requirements to restrict access and require user verification are included

While these surveys may be completed using email, Microsoft Word, or Microsoft Excel®, it is much more convenient to use a tool such as OneTrust to facilitate collation and rollup of responses.

In Figure 8.2, the OneTrust questionnaire asks whether the recipient sends emails as part of a marketing campaign. If the answer is "no," the risk is low; otherwise, it is medium. If the recipient does send emails as part of a marketing campaign, the recipient is asked to describe the risks and catalog the situation in terms of any risk mitigants.

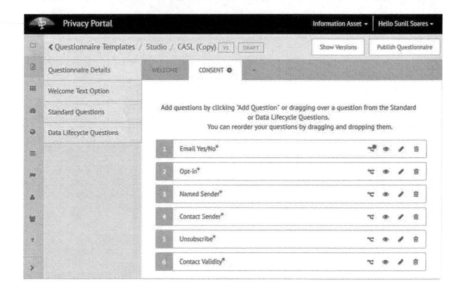

Figure 8.1: Sample CASL survey in OneTrust

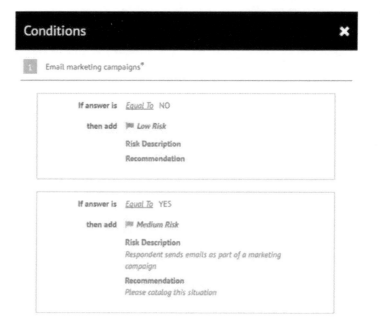

Figure 8.2: CASL questionnaire determining risk in OneTrust

Question 2 in OneTrust specifically asks respondents to indicate whether they are only sending unsolicited emails as part of a marketing campaign whose recipients have specifically opted in to the program. Question 3 elicits a response on whether the emails clearly name the sender or the person on whose behalf the emails were sent (Figure 8.3).

Figure 8.3: OneTrust CASL questions about marketing campaigns

OneTrust supports overall risk reporting based on responses from survey respondents. For example, in Figure 8.4, the GDPR Readiness Assessment survey highlights a risk that the organization collects special categories of data (race and ethnicity) to support Anti-Money Laundering (AML) compliance.

Risk ▼	Project Name	Project Status	Risk Description	Risk Recommendation	Risk Status	Section Name	Question Name	Question Answer	Justification
▲	GDPR Readiness Assessment	Completed	We collect race and ethnicity to comply with AML compliance.	N/A	Recommendation Added	General	Collect Special Categories	Yes	

Figure 8.4: OneTrust overall risk readiness reporting
to support regulations

Conduct Vendor Risk Assessments

Assessing the risk of any vendors providing services for the handling of sensitive data in an organization is very important. Regulations are increasingly mandating formalized vendor risk management. Any processing activities performed by vendors should be subject to vendor risk assessments. GDPR Article 30 contains requirements for maintaining records of processing activities[7]:

GDPR Article 30(2-4)

Records of Processing Activities

2. Each processor and, where applicable, the processor's representative shall maintain a record of all categories of processing activities carried out on behalf of a controller, containing:

  (a) the name and contact details of the processor or processors and of each controller on behalf of which the processor is acting, and, where applicable, of the controller's or the processor's representative, and the data protection officer;

  (b) the categories of processing carried out on behalf of each controller;

  (c) where applicable, transfers of personal data to a third country or an international organization, including the identification of that third country or international organization and, in the case of transfers referred to in the second subparagraph of Article 49(1), the documentation of appropriate safeguards;

  (d) where possible, a general description of the technical and organizational security measures referred to in Article 32(1).

3. The records referred to in paragraphs 30(1) and 30(2) shall be in writing, including in electronic form.

4. The controller or the processor and, where applicable, the controller's or the processor's representative, shall make the record available to the supervisory authority on request.

---

[7] EU GDPR Article 30, "Records of processing activities," http://www.privacy-regulation.eu/en/30.htm.

Vendor Risk Management Programs

Vendor risk assessments and the development of vendor risk management programs can support attestation of regulatory adherence to the supervisory authorities and mitigate the risks associated with using third parties as well as the potential impact of fines or sensitive-information breaches. Both vendor organizational and technological vulnerabilities need to be identified to minimize data sovereignty exposure. Conducting vendor risk assessments can help an organization to achieve a desired outcome and avoid potential malicious acts or human error. Prudent vendor risk management programs should have a process for conducting initial risk assessments as well as periodic assessments/questionnaires.

Components of a vendor risk assessment include information gathering on areas such as:

- Vendor storage and transmission of sensitive data

- Cloud data segregation

- Subcontracted data processes

- Vendor access to data (remote access, administrative privileges, monitoring, and audit logs)

- Details of data protection (privacy and security) mechanisms

- Data loss prevention (DLP) processes

- Disaster recovery and business continuity plans

- Roles and responsibilities of any vendor-appointed staffing

- Knowledge of regulations and compliance capabilities and effectiveness

- Potential cybersecurity incident and potential breach response/communication processes

The use of a risk assessment template can drive a consistent methodology and criteria against which multiple vendors can be assessed. Questionnaire templates can also help to effectively target the right questions to the right people, to deliver the information necessary to perform a thorough assessment.

Results gathered from risk assessments can also be used to create a risk matrix to identify areas where regulatory compliance is strong, as well as areas that need improvement or where audit controls may be on the weak side. Upon analysis of the assessment results, the focus needs to remain on mitigating all identified risks. Implementing a published risk assessment process, which might include assessment results by vendor, rollups by area of risk, and assessment trends, can really help organizations systematically scrutinize how vendors manage protected data on their behalf.

Risk Management Standards

The International Organization for Standardization (ISO) has published several standards applicable to data security and risk management; ISO 27005 provides guidance for conducting formal data security risk assessments. The U.S. National Institute of Standards and Technology (NIST) provides guidance for risk management as well as risk assessments. Organizations can also use the Operationally Critical Threat, Asset, and Vulnerability Evaluation[SM] (OCTAVE[®]) method for assessment. Using OCTAVE, organizations leverage current security practices to assess the maturity of security practices within the organization.

The Payment Card Industry's (PCI's) Security Standards Council has published a risk assessment guideline geared toward credit card companies to assess the categories of risks and produce a matrix of vulnerability ratings. The standards break down third-party risk management into three categories: introduce risk, manage risk, and share risk. In determining the type of risk of your vendor, it is important to clearly define and understand the business relationship. Once risk assessments are performed, an organization can clearly make decisions regarding the value of vendor relationships versus the risk of maintaining them.[8]

Vendor Risk Management Software

There are some vendor risk management software tools on the market today to help assess the risk of partnering with vendors. These tools help automate the process of managing relationships with vendors and vendor risk. Some of the benefits of these tools include the ability to keep up with constantly evolving regulatory requirements; providing efficiencies for vendor contract management and contract reviews; incident and issue management; automated vendor surveys, questionnaires, and/or risk assessments; scoring and evaluating of vendor risks; vendor services

---

[8] PCI Security Standards Council, *PCI Data Security Standard (PCI DSS)*, https://www.pcisecuritystandards.org/documents/PCI_DSS_Risk_Assmt_Guidelines_v1.pdf.

analytics via key performance indicators (KPIs) and dashboards (e.g., risk ratings, service level agreement adherence, regulatory adherence); and audit facilitation. Current vendor risk management software providers include BWise®, LogicManager™, MetricStream™, Quantivate, and VendorINSIGHT®.

Summary

Data sovereignty regulations often require data protection impact assessments before introducing a new data set, process, or technology to the organization. These assessments can be performed using Microsoft Word or Excel or using a packaged application. Equally important are vendor risk assessments, which should be used to assess the risk of vendors providing services for the handling of an organization's sensitive data. Legislative provisions increasingly require formalized vendor risk management.

9

Data Lineage

Regulation sample	Description
Hong Kong Personal Data Privacy Ordinance, Section 33	Prohibition against transfer of personal data except in specified circumstances— "A data user shall not transfer personal data to a place outside Hong Kong. . . ."
European Union General Data Protection Regulation, Article 17(1)	Right to erasure ("right to be forgotten")— "The data subject shall have the right to obtain from the controller the erasure of personal data concerning him or her without undue delay and the controller shall have the obligation to erase personal data without undue delay where one of the following grounds applies. . . ."
European Union General Data Protection Regulation, Article 22(1)	Automated individual decision-making, including profiling— "The data subject shall have the right not to be subject to a decision based solely on automated processing, including profiling, which produces legal effects concerning him or her or similarly significantly affects him or her."
Singapore Personal Data Protection Act, Act 59(1)	Preservation of secrecy— "Subject to subsection (5), every specified person shall preserve, and aid in the preservation of, secrecy with regard to — (a) any personal data an organization would be required or authorized to refuse to disclose if it were contained in personal data requested under section 21. . . ."
Australian Privacy Act of 1988, Principle 8.1	Cross border disclosure of personal information— "Before an APP entity discloses personal information about an individual to a person (the overseas recipient). . . ."
Laws of Malaysia Personal Data Protection Act 2010, Act 709, Section 44(1)	Record to be kept by data user— "A data user shall keep and maintain a record of any application, notice, request, or any other information relating to personal data that has been or is being processed by him."

Data lineage provides transparency as well as an audit trail for tracking data from source to target. Data lineage pertains to both business- and technical-related lineage and is a critical component of compliance with data sovereignty regulations.

Article 30 of the GDPR requires organizations to maintain a record of processing activities. This record must include a description of the categories of personal data; the categories of recipients of personal data, including those in third countries or international organizations; and transfers of personal data to a third country or an international organization. The recordkeeping requirements also extend to so-called processors who process data on behalf of an organization.

Section 44 of Malaysia's Personal Data Protection Act (Record to be kept by data user) indicates that organizations must keep and maintain records of applications, notices, and requests for personal data that have been processed. Article 17 of the GDPR (Right to erasure ('right to be forgotten')) requires organizations to have visibility into every system and associated file where a person's data may be stored, in the event that the data subject requests it to be erased. This includes backup files and copies of the data.

To comply with these requirements, data governance teams need to strengthen metadata management and data lineage capabilities.

Show Data Flows with Horizontal Data Lineage

Data governance teams need to be able to demonstrate data flows in the form of horizontal data lineage from source applications to target applications. Tools such as IBM InfoSphere Information Governance Catalog support this capability. Figure 9.1 shows the lineage of the EMPLOYEE/FIRSTNME field through multiple IBM InfoSphere DataStage® jobs from several back-end databases.

Show Data Flows with Vertical Data Lineage

Data governance teams need to be able to demonstrate data flows in the form of vertical data lineage from a business term to the associated data artifacts. Figure 9.2 shows the details of a business term, Date of Birth, that is defined in IBM InfoSphere Information Governance Catalog. This business term is located with the Customer data category. Jack Smith is the data owner, and Jill Duffy is the data steward. Date of Birth is associated with several data quality rules, including MDMP-BR-0211; these rules are critical to an overall data governance program but may be

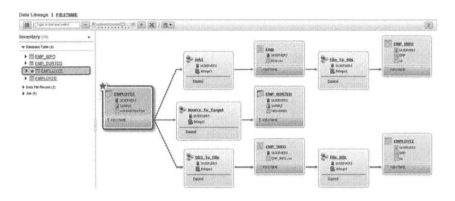

Figure 9.1: IBM InfoSphere Information Governance Catalog
with detailed lineage

📋 Date Of Birth

Date on which the person was born

Parent Category	📋 Business Terms » 📋 Customer
Labels (1)	🔖 Member CDE
Stewards (2)	🗂 Data Owner Jack Smith , 🗂 Data Steward Jill Duffy
Status	Standard
Governed by Rules (4)	🏷 MDMP-BR-0211
	🏷 MDMP-BR-0700
	🏷 MDMP-BR-1404
	🏷 MDMP-BR-1415

▼ General Information

Acceptable Use Standards	Customer age cannot be shared with third parties without approval from the customer.
CDE	Yes
CDE Tier	1
Is Modifier	False
Type	None

▶ Associated Terms

▼ Assigned Assets (4)

Assigned Assets (4)	🗂 BIRTHDATE / 🖥 Model1 - Logical » 🖥 EMPLOYEE
	📄 BIRTHDATE / 📄 IASERVER3 » 🖥 SAMPLE » 🖥 ADMINISTRATOR » 🖥 EMPLOYEE
	📄 BIRTHDATE
	📄 birthdate / 📄 IASERVER3 » 🖥 hive2 » 🖥 default » 🖥 employee

Figure 9.2: IBM InfoSphere Information Governance Catalog
lineage of the business term Date of Birth

less important from a data sovereignty perspective. The acceptable use standard states that customer age cannot be shared with third parties without approval from the customer. Date of Birth has been classified as a tier 1 critical data element. Finally, the business term has been mapped to four instances of technical metadata in four applications.

The data governance team can also use Collibra to map Social Security number to the SOC_NM column in the Workday (WD) application and the SOC_NUM column in the Tax Management (TM) application (Figure 9.3).

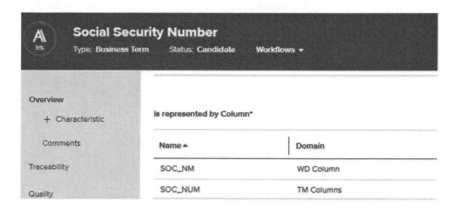

Figure 9.3: Mapping of CDEs in Collibra to source data elements

Summary

Data sovereignty regulations require organizations to maintain traceability of all activities related to the processing of data. These regulations also apply to the organization and any vendor or third party that participates in the processing of a data subject's personal data. Using data flow diagrams and data mappings, an organization can successfully provide evidence of the lineage of data from source to target.

10

Information Lifecycle Management, End User Computing, and Data Quality

Regulation sample	Description
Russian Federal Law 152-FZ, Article 14(1)	Personal data subject's right to access his personal data— "The subject of personal data have the right to require the operator to clarify his personal data, their blocking or destruction if personal data are incomplete, outdated, inaccurate, or obtained illegally, are not necessary for the stated purpose of the processing, as well as to take measures prescribed by law for the protection of their rights."
European Union General Data Protection Regulation, Article 16	Right to rectification— ". . .the data subject shall have the right to have incomplete personal data completed. . . ."
European Union General Data Protection Regulation, Article 17(2)	Right to erasure ("right to be forgotten")— "Where the controller has made the personal data public and is obliged pursuant to paragraph 1 to erase the personal data, the controller, taking account of available technology and the cost of implementation, shall take reasonable steps, including technical measures, to inform controllers which are processing the personal data that the data subject has requested the erasure by such controllers of any links to, or copy or replication of, those personal data."
European Union General Data Protection Regulation, Recital 85	Addressing personal data breach— ". . .Therefore, as soon as the controller becomes aware that a personal data breach has occurred, the controller should notify the personal data breach to the supervisory authority without undue delay and, where feasible, not later than 72 hours after having become aware of it, unless the controller is able to demonstrate, in accordance with the accountability principle, that the personal data breach is unlikely to result in a risk to the rights and freedoms of natural persons. . . ."

Continued

Regulation sample	Description
European Union General Data Protection Regulation, Article 19	Notification obligation regarding rectification or erasure of personal data or restriction of processing— "The controller shall communicate any rectification or erasure of personal data or restriction of processing carried out in accordance with Article 16, Article 17(1) and Article 18 to each recipient to whom the personal data have been disclosed, unless this proves impossible or involves disproportionate effort. The controller shall inform the data subject about those recipients if the data subject requests it."
Singapore Personal Data Protection Act, Act 89(4)	Preservation of secrecy— "Every claim made under subsection (3) shall be supported by a written statement giving reasons why the information is confidential."
Singapore Personal Data Protection Act, Act 22(1)	Correction of personal data— "An individual may request an organization to correct an error or omission in the personal data about the individual that is in the possession or under the control of the organization."
Singapore Personal Data Protection Act, Act 23	Accuracy of personal data— "An organization shall make a reasonable effort to ensure that personal data collected by or on behalf of the organization is accurate and complete. . . ."
Australian Privacy Act of 1988, Principle 10.1	Quality of personal information— "An APP entity must take such steps (if any) as are reasonable in the circumstances to ensure that the personal information that the entity collects is accurate, up to date, and complete."
Australian Privacy Act of 1988, Principle 13.1	Correction of personal information— ". . .the entity must take such steps (if any) as are reasonable in the circumstances to correct that information to ensure that, having regard to the purpose for which it is held, the information is accurate, up to date, complete, relevant, and not misleading."
Australian Privacy Act of 1988, Principle 12.1	Access to personal information— "If an APP entity holds personal information about an individual, the entity must, on request by the individual, give the individual access to the information."
Australian Privacy Act of 1988, Principle 2.1	Anonymity and pseudonymity— "Individuals must have the option of not identifying themselves, or of using a pseudonym, when dealing with an APP entity in relation to a particular matter."
Hong Kong Personal Data Privacy Ordinance, Chapter 486, Part V, Section 22(1)	Data correction request— ". . .[where] the data subject considers that the data are inaccurate, then that individual or relevant person, as the case may be, may make a request that the data user make the necessary correction to the data."

In this chapter, we focus on information lifecycle management, end user computing, and data quality, all of which are critical elements in meeting the demands of data sovereignty requirements.

Information Lifecycle Management

Information lifecycle management (ILM) refers to a systematic, policy-based approach to information architecture, classification, collection, use, archival, retention, and deletion. ILM covers records, structured and unstructured data, and business- and IT-managed content regardless of their location, format, and media. Data sovereignty laws require organizations to have clearly defined data retention, archival, and destruction processes primarily for critical sensitive or protected data.

With the growing use of cloud computing and multifaceted data storage and retention strategies, successfully managing and executing your information lifecycle policies while complying with data sovereignty laws can be quite challenging. Data subject rights have been significantly enhanced with recent updates to data protection laws globally. For example, the GDPR's right to erasure ("right to be forgotten") provisions have been enhanced significantly; organizations are now required to erase personal data, and in the event that the data was made public, the organizations processing the data must inform the data subjects and, if requested, erase any links to, copies of, or replicas of the data. GDPR Article 5(1)(e) also states that personal data shall be kept in a form that permits identification of data subjects for no longer than is necessary for the purposes for which the personal data are processed. The regulation has instituted a subject access request where the organizations must provide information regarding their processing, export solutions, and storage limits in electronic form.

Legal and compliance teams must stay abreast of data sovereignty regulations to successfully identify the relevant exemptions under each jurisdictional regulation and determine how each can be applied where desired. An assessment of how the rights trigger and will be implemented in all contexts will need to occur, followed by applying mechanisms to search for, filter, and separate the information to be compliant with data sovereignty regulations.

Organizations may want to explore opportunities to engage with third-party vendors for a variety of business reasons. Data suppliers, for example, offer services to enhance data portability in relation to the regulations of personal data. Testing and validation resources can lower costs and reduce unauthorized access to internal protected data. When engaging with these vendors, it is important to maintain data sharing agreements and ensure that legal has reviewed the contract to ensure there is no chance of a data breach under any data sovereignty law.

End User Computing

Information lifecycle management also includes the management of end user computing (EUC). EUCs can be any spreadsheets, documents, queries, scripts, or other solutions that are created to fulfill a business, financial, or operational need on a recurring basis. Most often, these solutions are developed outside the information technology environment. There is no dedicated IT support team, and the solutions do not follow IT change management processes. Data sovereignty regulations require organizations to have a sound inventory of their sensitive data even if it resides in spreadsheets and Microsoft Access® databases.

Any data that is a part of EUC processing must be encrypted, redacted, or tokenized in order to comply with data sovereignty regulations such as Australian Privacy Principle 2 (Anonymity and pseudonymity) or Singapore's Personal Data Protection Act 59 (Preservation of secrecy).

Tools such as ClusterSeven give organizations the ability to manage an inventory of EUCs. These tools also provide the capability to scan the infrastructure for Excel files and Access databases, which can then be cataloged in the EUC inventory.

Data Quality and Rectification

Data quality management is a discipline that includes methods to measure and improve the quality and integrity of an organization's data. Data quality management is foundational to data governance programs, while data rectification is a component of necessary compliance with data sovereignty regulations.

Although your organization needs to maintain high levels of data quality to satisfy an effective data governance program, to satisfy data sovereignty requirements we speak of the exercise as data rectification, and/or data erasure.

Some examples of data rectification and data erasure laws include the following:

- *GDPR*—Article 16 (Right to rectification) states that the data subject shall have the right to obtain from the controller, without any undue delay, the rectification of any inaccurate personal data concerning him or her. The data subject shall have the right to have incomplete personal data completed.

- *GDPR*—Article 17 (Right to erasure ("right to be forgotten")) states that the data subject shall have the right to obtain from the controller the erasure of personal data concerning him or her without undue delay, if the data is no longer relevant to the original purpose for which it was collected, if the data subject objects to the processing, or if the processing was unlawful.

- *Singapore Personal Data Protection Act*—Act 22 (Correction of personal data) states that an individual may ask an organization to correct an error or omission in the personal data about the individual that is in the possession or under the control of the organization, and that the organization shall correct the personal data as soon as practical. Furthermore, any corrected data must be sent to every other organization to which the personal data was disclosed by the organization within a year before the date the correction was made, unless that other organization does not need the corrected personal data for any legal or business purpose.

- *Australian Privacy Principles*—APP 10 (Quality of personal information) states, in paragraphs 10.1 and 10.2, that an entity must take such steps (if any) as are reasonable under the circumstances to ensure that the personal information that the entity collects (10.1) and that the entity uses or discloses (10.2) is, with regard to the purpose of the use or disclosure, accurate, up-to-date, complete, and relevant.

To comply with regulatory requirements for data rectification and erasure, data governance teams need to implement controls, which are made up of detailed procedures to enable customers, employees, and other data subjects to address data quality issues relating to their information in a timely manner. These controls would then be measured against defined business rules to determine the quality of the data (e.g., data quality dimensions of completeness, accuracy, and consistency). Table 10.1 lists some data quality dimensions and illustrates how they can be used to create data quality rules.

Table 10.1: Data quality dimensions		
Data quality dimension	Definition	Sample data quality rule
Completeness	The degree to which data elements are populated	Employee ID cannot be NULL.
Conformity	The degree to which data elements correspond to expected formats or valid values or ranges of values	State should be from the agreed-upon list of code values for state.
Consistency	The degree of relational integrity between data elements and other data elements	The customer "opt-in" email flag expiration date should be greater than or equal to the "opt-in" email flag effective date.
Synchronization	The degree to which data elements are consistent from one data store to the next	Customer ID in the master data hub must be the same as the one in the EUC customer file stored on the business database.
Uniqueness	The degree to which data elements are unique within a data store	Customer IDs should be unique in the customer reference table.
Timeliness	The degree to which data is available on a timely basis	Patient covered lives must be calculated by 10 a.m. Eastern time Monday to Friday.
Accuracy	The degree to which data elements are accurate	Customer NAICS code must be accurate.

Data sovereignty laws have encouraged data subjects to take accountability for the accuracy of their data that is collected, stored, and transferred. To increase transparency, your organization may want to consider creating a self-service portal where data subjects can view their data and request updates, corrections, or termination of their data. Legal and compliance can work with the technology teams to ensure that the functionality of the mechanism meets timeframes outlined in the regulations.

Summary

Data sovereignty laws require organizations to have clearly defined data retention, archival, and destruction processes primarily for critical sensitive or protected data. Data subject rights have been enhanced with emerging and redefined data protection laws. Legal and compliance teams must stay abreast of data sovereignty regulations to successfully identify the relevant exemptions under each jurisdictional regulation and determine how each can be applied where desired.

Instituting a robust information lifecycle management program is beneficial to an organization's data sovereignty goals. Most end user computing solutions are developed outside the information technology environment, where there is no dedicated IT support team and no change management processes.

Data sovereignty regulations require organizations to have a sound inventory of their sensitive data even if that data resides in spreadsheets and Microsoft Access databases. Data rectification and erasure is a crucial component of data quality to support compliance with data sovereignty regulations.

Data sovereignty laws have encouraged data subjects to take accountability for the accuracy of their data that is collected, stored, and transferred. For compliance with data sovereignty regulatory requirements, the data governance team should implement controls to address data quality issues relating to data subjects' rights for data rectification and erasure.

11

Model Governance

Regulation sample	Description
France Data Protection Act, Article 8.7	Statistical processing— ". . .Statistical processing carried out by the National Institute for Statistics and Economic Studies or one of the ministerial statistical services, in compliance with Law No. 51-711 of 7 June 1951 on the obligation, coordination, and secrecy in statistics after consultation with the National Council for Statistical Information and under the conditions laid down in Article 25 of this Law. . . ."
France Data Protection Act, Article 10	Decisions based on automated processing— "No judicial decision involving an assessment of a person's conduct may be based on an automated processing of personal data intended to evaluate certain aspects of his personality. No other decision which has legal effects in relation to a person can be taken solely on the basis of an automated processing of data intended to define the profile of the person concerned or to assess certain aspects of his personality. . . ."
European Union General Data Protection Regulation, Article 21(1)	Right to object— "The data subject shall have the right to object, on grounds relating to his or her particular situation, at any time to processing of personal data concerning him or her which is based on point (e) or (f) of Article 6(1), including profiling based on those provisions. . . ."

Model governance is a comprehensive discipline that improves the trust-worthiness and regulatory compliance of statistical models. Statistical models may be used for a variety of reasons within marketing, employment, and risk management. For example, the marketing department in a bank may use statistical models to identify prospects for credit card offers. The human resources department may use models to identify candidates who are most likely to succeed. Statistical models are sometimes referred to as propensity or predictive models.

Similar to data governance, model governance has several subdisciplines, including the following:

- *Model ownership*—This includes the name of the model owner to enforce accountability for the results of the models.

- *Model metadata management*—This includes a comprehensive model catalog, including details regarding name, creation date, methodology, input variables, and output variables.

- *Model quality management*—This includes processes to validate the results of models on an ongoing basis.

- *Model acceptable use*—This includes the processes to ensure that the models are used in a manner consistent with business policies and regulatory requirements.

Model governance teams need to observe certain best practices to support compliance with data sovereignty laws.

Maintain Model Metadata

Organizations should have a comprehensive inventory of all statistical models for product, business, or customer interactions. This catalog should capture, at a minimum, the details of the model methodology, tool and application interfaces, name, owner, purpose, inputs, outputs, and creation and validation dates. This catalog, or metadata, can be captured using the template in Table 11.1.

Table 11.1: Template for model metadata	
Attribute	**Description**
Model ID	Unique identifier for the model
Name	Name of the model
Description	Description of the model
Business purpose	Business use of the model
Methodology	Methodology used to develop the model (e.g., regression analysis, rules, logistic regression, random forest)
Application	Application used to develop the model (e.g., SAS®, R™, Hadoop®)
Level 1 model category	Name of the Level 1 category where the model can be best classified

Level 2 model category	Name of the Level 2 category where the model can be best classified, if applicable
Report and line item	Name of the line item in any report to which the model applies
Input variables	Names of the variables used as inputs into the models
Input models	IDs of models that are used as input into this model
Business rules governing inputs	Business rules that govern variable and model inputs into this model
Output variables	Names of the variables that are outputs from this model
Dependent models	IDs of models that depend on the outputs of this model
Business rules governing outputs	Business rules that govern the outputs of this model
Model creator	Name of individual who created the model
Model creator department	Department of individual who created the model
Model owner	Name of individual who owns the model
Model owner department	Department of individual who owns the model
Model creation date	Date that the model was created
Model deployment date	Date that the model was deployed
Model validation date	Date that the model was independently validated or will be validated
Model validation owner	Name of the individual who independently validated or will validate the model
Model validation department	Department of the individual who independently validated or will validate the model

Validate Acceptable Use of Model Inputs

Model governance should adopt acceptable use standards to determine what data may be used as inputs into models. For example, when engaging in data analytics, U.S. companies should consider U.S. federal equal opportunity laws, including the Age Discrimination in Employment Act, the Americans with Disabilities Act, the Equal Credit Opportunity Act, the Fair Credit Reporting Act, the Fair Housing Act, the Genetic Information Nondiscrimination Act, and Title VII of the Civil Rights Act of 1964. These laws prohibit discrimination based on protected characteristics such as race, color, sex or gender, religion, age, disability status, national origin, marital status, and genetic information.

With some exceptions, Article 9 of the GDPR prohibits the processing of personal data that reveals racial or ethnic origin, political opinions, religious or philosophical beliefs, or trade-union membership, as well as the processing of genetic or biometric data for the purpose of uniquely identifying a natural person. The processing of health-related data or data about a natural person's sex life or sexual orientation is also prohibited.

In most instances, model governance teams should establish controls to ensure that prohibited data is not used within models. However, there may be instances where use of this data may be required in order to comply with other regulations. For example, certain data types may be required to comply with Anti-Money Laundering (AML) laws. In these cases, model governance teams need to obtain approval from legal, privacy, and compliance departments prior to the use of any prohibited data in their models.

Validate Acceptable Use of Model Outputs

Data sovereignty laws often require organizations to review the outputs of analytical models to reduce the likelihood of any unintended consequences. For example, Article 22 of the GDPR deals with automated individual decision-making, including profiling. Going back to the topic in Chapter 6, "disparate treatment" or "disparate impact," model governance teams must be aware of the consequences of their actions on customers and employees.

Under such an analysis, a company that avoids, for example, expressly screening job applicants based on gender and instead uses big data analytics to screen applicants in a way that has a disparate impact on women may still be subject to certain equal employment opportunity laws, if the screening does not serve a legitimate business need or if the need can reasonably be achieved by another means with a smaller disparate impact.

Let's consider a bank that uses U.S. ZIP codes in its analytical models to make credit offers to customers. The use of ZIP codes may result in disparate impact if the bank excludes certain ZIP codes that have a preponderance of minorities. An acceptable use data standard may state that the bank may use ZIP codes in its analytical models, but the results must be reviewed independently to ensure that they do not result in a disparate impact on a protected class.[1]

---

[1] U.S. Federal Trade Commission, *Big Data: A Tool for Inclusion or Exclusion*, January 2016, https://www.ftc.gov/system/files/documents/reports/big-data-tool-inclusion-or-exclusion-understanding-issues/160106big-data-rpt.pdf.

Summary

Model governance is a comprehensive discipline that improves the trustworthiness and regulatory compliance of statistical models. Data sovereignty laws require organizations to develop strong model governance programs, including metadata management and reviewing the acceptable use of inputs and outputs.

12

Data Sharing Agreements

Regulation sample	Description
Singapore Personal Data Protection Act, Act 26(1)	Transfer of personal data outside Singapore— "An organization shall not transfer any personal data to a country or territory outside Singapore except in accordance with requirements prescribed under this Act. . . ."
European Union General Data Protection Regulation, Article 44	General principle for transfers— "Any transfer of personal data which are undergoing processing or are intended for processing after transfer to a third country or to an international organization shall take place only if. . .the conditions laid down in this Chapter are complied with by the controller and processor, including for onward transfers of personal data from the third country or an international organization to another third country or to another international organization. . . ."
European Union General Data Protection Regulation, Article 50	International cooperation for the protection of personal data— ". . .(a) develop international cooperation mechanisms to facilitate the effective enforcement of legislation for the protection of personal data; (b) provide international mutual assistance in the enforcement of legislation for the protection of personal data, including through notification, complaint referral, investigative assistance and information exchange, subject to appropriate safeguards for the protection of personal data and other fundamental rights and freedoms;. . . ."
Australian Privacy Act of 1988, Principle 8	Cross-border disclosure of personal information— "Before an APP entity discloses personal information about an individual to a person (the overseas recipient): (a) who is not in Australia or an external Territory; and (b) who is not the entity or the individual; the entity must take such steps as are reasonable in the circumstances to ensure that the overseas recipient does not breach the Australian Privacy Principles (other than Australian Privacy Principle 1) in relation to the information."

Continued

Regulation sample	Description
Russian Federal Law 152-FZ, Article 12(3)	Cross-border transfer of personal data— "The operator must ensure that the foreign State on the territory of which the transfer of personal data adequately protected personal data subject's rights, prior to the implementation of the cross-border transfer of personal data. . . ."
Hong Kong Personal Data Privacy Ordinance, Chapter 486, Section 33(2)	Prohibition against transfer of personal data except in specified circumstances— "A data user shall not transfer personal data to a place outside Hong Kong unless (a) the place is specified for the purposes of this section in a notice under subsection (3). . . ."
Laws of Malaysia Personal Data Protection Act 2010, Act 709, Section 129(1)	Transfer of personal data to places outside of Malaysia— "A data user shall not transfer any personal data of a data subject to a place outside Malaysia unless to such place as specified by the Minister, upon the recommendation of the Commissioner, by notification published in the Gazette. . . ."
German Federal Data Protection Act, Section 4b(1)	Transfer of personal data abroad and to supranational or international bodies— "The transfer of personal data to bodies. . .shall be subject to Section 15(1), Section 16(1), and Sections 28 to 30a in accordance with the laws and agreements applicable to such transfer, in so far as transfer is effected in connection with activities which fall in part or in their entirety within the scope of the law of the European Communities."
Canada Personal Information Protected and Electronic Documents, Section 1, Subsection 9(1)	When access is prohibited— ". . .an organization shall not give an individual access to personal information if doing so would likely reveal personal information about a third party. . . ."

Data protection, privacy, and sovereignty strictly regulate the sharing and transfer of personal data. It is critical for any personal information being shared or transferred across borders to be clearly documented and approved by legal and compliance teams. In most cases, cross-border data transfers may be made only if the transfer is made to an adequate jurisdiction (declared by regulatory commissions). Data sharing and underlying data movements can be used to manage, track, and audit the movement of critical data.

Data sharing agreements are contracts that govern the sharing of data between two entities. These entities may be divisions of the same company or distinct legal entities. Data sharing agreements can also be contracts between platforms or application stakeholders. Intracompany agreements are not legally enforceable but may be subject to internal audit review. On the other hand, intercompany agreements may be legally binding. Data sharing agreements cover topics such as the list of attributes being shared, the country of origin and country of destination, acceptable use standards, and restrictions on how data may be further propagated downstream.

Organizations should establish data sharing agreements for the internal and external dissemination of critical information. These agreements govern the sharing of data and information between applications, vendors, and businesses while capturing helpful metadata.

Data sharing agreements and data movement agreements have similar functionality but have key differences. Data sharing agreements are better suited to data attestations and cross-border transfer requirements, as well as enforcing acceptable use of information in downstream applications. Data movement agreements provide the organizing vehicle to tie physical data elements to consuming systems and track which movements contain sensitive personal data.

Establish Template for Data Sharing Agreements

The data governance team should use a template for data sharing agreements to support the acceptable use, security, and restrictions of data being passed between data owners. Table 12.1 provides an example of such a template, and Table 12.2 shows a sample data sharing agreement.

Table 12.1: Sample template for data sharing agreement	
Attribute	**Description**
Name	One-sentence description of the data sharing agreement
Type of data being shared	High-level description of the types of data included in the agreement (e.g., nature of personal data, purpose, and duration of processing)
Acceptable use	How the consuming system can use the data (i.e., approved guidelines for data once it has been persisted by the consuming system, who has access to it, what they can do with it)
Restricted additional sharing	Restrictions on how data may be shared with downstream consumers, used to derive new data, or propagated to other systems
Country of origin	Country in which the data originated
Country of destination	Country to which the data is being transferred
	Continued

Attribute	Description
Consuming system/application	Name of the system/application that is consuming the data being shared
Consuming data owner	Name and title of the data owner who consumes the information (e.g., John Doe, CFO)
Producing system/application	Name of the system/application that is producing the data being shared
Producing data owner	Name and title of the data owner who produces the information (e.g., Jill Smith, CRO)
Critical data elements	Name of the fields in the report to which the data sharing agreement applies
Associated data feed(s)	Names of associated data feeds or web services that provide data or access to data supported by the specific parameters of this data sharing agreement
Define data quality responsibility	Consuming and producing parties' involvement in validating state of data and mitigation for materially altered data
Consuming system accountabilities	Accountabilities of the consuming system for ensuring data security (e.g., compliance with third parties, application of business rules)
Retention	How long the data in the data sharing agreement is allowed to be retained by the customer
Effective date	Effective date of the data sharing agreement

Table 12.2: Sample data sharing agreement	
Attribute	**Description**
Name	Customer Contact Details
Type of data being shared	Current customer personal contact details for marketing campaigns
Acceptable use	Data may only be used to contact customers who meet profile and demographic targets and who have opted to receive marketing information for legally approved marketing campaigns. Acceptable use of this critical data has been reviewed and approved by the legal, risk, and compliance offices. Use of data must adhere to approved acceptable uses, and comply with the identifiable legal basis for consent/use, processing, and transfer of personal data (EU GDPR Article 44).
Restricted additional sharing	Data may not be propagated from the consuming system to any other downstream systems or shared in any other format outside this data sharing agreement as defined.
Country of origin	France

Country of destination	Belgium
Consuming system/application	Customer Digital Platform
Consuming data owner	Joe Bloggs – SVP – Marketing
Producing system/application	Customer Profile
Producing data owner	Jean Dupont – VP – Data Strategy
Critical data elements	First name, last name, customer ID, home address, personal email address, opt-in status, relationship type, marketing segment code
Associated data feed(s)	Cust_Profile – on-demand outbound web service
Define data quality responsibility	Data quality is the responsibility of the producer; as such, the Customer Digital Platform relies on Customer Profile for the completeness and accuracy of data. All critical data elements should meet established quality thresholds.
Consuming system accountabilities	Consuming system is accountable for securing data in accordance with the company's information security policies. Consumer must comply with any legislative data protection/privacy/sovereignty regulations applicable in the destination country.
Retention	Data must be replaced with each new feed and can only be used within two hours of feed.
Effective date	2017-15-01

Data sharing agreements must lay out the responsibilities of the consuming division to comply with acceptable use standards for data that is being shared. This is especially important for personally identifiable information (PII) and other sensitive data. Data sharing agreements can be associated with model contracts, intercompany data transfer agreements, and data usage agreements to comply with data sovereignty regulations. It is important to capture what data is being shared, where the data is being transferred, and how the data can be used:

- List attributes being shared.
- Define acceptable use standards for shared attributes.
- Identify the country of origin and country of destination.
- Define the responsibility for data quality.
- List restrictions on how data may be shared with downstream consumers or used to derive new data.
- Tie physical data elements to consuming systems.

The Australian Privacy Act, EU GDPR, and Singapore PDPA require organizations to safeguard data and regulate the transfer of data internally and externally to the country's border. Using tools such as Collibra, organizations can identify and govern attributes, restrict the sharing, and tie physical elements to consuming systems while maintaining compliance with data sovereignty regulations (Figure 12.1).

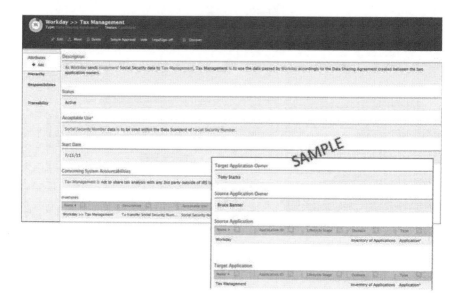

Figure 12.1: Data sharing agreement in Collibra

Summary

Data sharing agreements govern the data shared between entities and across borders. They provide a formalized structure around managing and tracking the movement of critical personal data elements, auditing their security, and enforcing acceptable use of information in downstream applications. Data sharing agreements must lay out the responsibilities of the consuming division to comply with acceptable use standards for data that is being shared and must hold data owners on both the producing and consuming ends accountable.

13

Monitoring and Enforcement of Controls

Regulation sample	Description
European Union General Data Protection Regulation, Article 40(3)	Codes of conduct— "In addition to adherence by controllers or processors subject to this Regulation, codes of conduct approved pursuant to paragraph 5 of this Article and having general validity pursuant to paragraph 9 of this Article may also be adhered to by controllers or processors that are not subject to this Regulation pursuant to Article 3 in order to provide appropriate safeguards within the framework of personal data transfers to third countries or international organizations. . . ."
France Data Protection Act, Article 44	Monitoring the implementation of treatments— "The members of the National Commission on Informatics and Civil Liberties and the officials of their services authorized under the conditions set out in the last paragraph of Article 19 shall have access from 6 a.m. to 9 p.m. for the exercise of their tasks, to places, premises, enclosures, installations, or establishments used for the processing of personal data and which are for professional use. . . ."
Canada Personal Information Protected and Electronic Documents, Section 2, Subsection 16	Remedies— "The Court may, in addition to any other remedies it may give, (a) order an organization to correct its practices in order to comply with sections 5 to 10; (b) order an organization to publish a notice of any action taken or proposed to be taken to correct its practices, whether or not ordered to correct them under paragraph (a); and (c) award damages to the complainant, including damages for any humiliation that the complainant has suffered."

Continued

Regulation sample	Description
Canada's Anti-Spam Law, Section 17(2)	Notice to produce— "The designated person may issue the notice only for the purpose of one or more of the following: (a) verifying compliance with this Act; (b) determining whether any of sections 6 to 9 has been contravened. . . ."
Canada's Anti-Spam Law, Section 40(1)	Enforcement— "A demand served under section 15, a notice served under section 17, an undertaking entered into under section 21, and an order of the Commission made under section 26 may be made an order of a court of competent jurisdiction and may be enforced in the same manner as an order of that court as if it had been an order of that court on the date it was served. . . ."
Russian Federal Law 152-FZ, Article 18.1	Measures aimed at ensuring the implementation of operator responsibilities stipulated by this federal law— ". . .the Government of the Russian Federation establishes a list of measures aimed at ensuring compliance with the obligations provided for in this federal law and adopted in accordance with the regulations, operators are State or municipal authorities. 4. the operator shall be obliged to submit documents and local acts specified in part 1 of this article, and (or) otherwise confirm the measures referred to in paragraph 1 of this article, upon request of the authorized body for the protection of the rights of subjects of personal data. . . ."
Russian Federal Law 152-FZ, Article 19	Measures to ensure the security of personal data processing— ". . .application of organizational and technical measures to ensure the security of personal data processing of personal data in information systems needed to comply with the protection of personal data, pursuant to which the Government of the Russian Federation provides levels of protection of personal data. . . ."

Regulatory Compliance

Governments have an easier time getting access to data if it is within their jurisdiction. Personal information sent outside a home country is subject to laws in the country to which it is being sent. The Australian Privacy Principles state that cloud service providers must disclose what information is being sent outside Australia. Organizations that lack the ability to protect the data that they collect, store, and transfer create potential risks to their corporate brand, face financial penalties for non-compliance, and can lose their right to operate in some countries.

Organizations must be able to demonstrate an ability to comply with data sovereignty regulations; provide evidence that processes are implemented, monitored, and enforced; and acknowledge and provide evidence of their ability to mitigate data breaches.

Collaboration

Data sovereignty compliance is larger than a single department in an organization. A choreographed effort involving data governance, legal, compliance, and technology teams must be actioned. Figure 13.1 shows the elements and interaction of an effective approach to ensuring that the appropriate controls are in place and adhered to:

- Have legal and compliance help dissect and interpret rapidly changing regulations.

- Conduct privacy impact assessments to assess security and privacy needs.

- Implement data protection practices.

- Gain better visibility of data sources, data stores, data lineage, and personal data usage.

- Manage data residency.

- Develop data sovereignty controls.

- Measure adherence.

Figure 13.1: Collaboration for data sovereignty compliance

Monitor Operational Risk Controls

Once an organization's legal team reviews published legislation that impacts the areas of the world where business is conducted or where customers and employees are serviced, it is necessary to determine the impact of the regulations on the organization's data landscape and to have an information governance framework in place to facilitate management and adherence. Data governance standards may be written to require the approval of legal and/or compliance for various tasks, such as communicating with customers, transferring data from one area of the world to another intracompany, and working with cloud providers and their contractors when transferring, storing, or processing information to reinforce alignment with data sovereignty regulations.

Collibra Data Governance Center supports an inventory of operational risk controls to support data sovereignty compliance. For example, GDPR Article 9 (Processing of special categories of personal data) restricts the use of special categories of data such as race and ethnic origin. However, banks may need to use restricted categories of data to support compliance with regulations such as Anti-Money Laundering (AML). Figure 13.2 displays an operational risk control in Collibra.

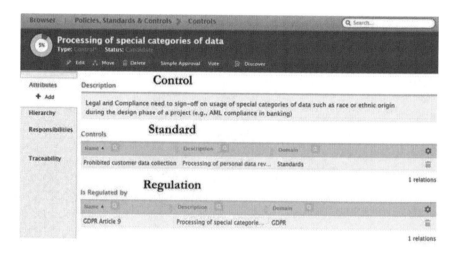

Figure 13.2: Data governance controls in Collibra to support data sovereignty

The control states that legal and compliance need to sign off on the use of restricted categories of data for specific purposes, such as AML compliance. The Collibra control is related to a broader data standard that deals with the collection of prohibited customer data. For referential integrity, the data governance team has included a reference to GDPR Article 9 as well.

The operational risk control may also be operationalized by a Collibra workflow as shown in Figure 13.3. This data governance workflow documents approvals by the relevant parties (stakeholders) prior to use of a new data set, such as clickstream data, in the design process.

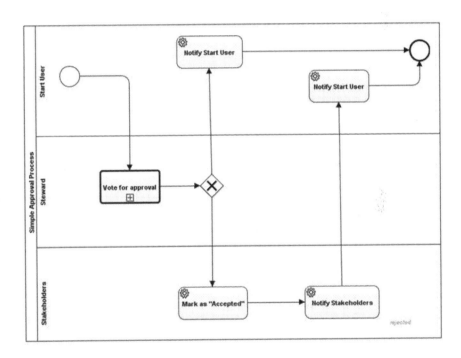

Figure 13.3: Workflow in Collibra

Data Governance Dashboards

As part of a framework of internal controls, companies should monitor and enforce the implementation of data policies, standards, and processes developed to meet the needs of data sovereignty requirements. An effective way to monitor compliance is through the use of data governance dashboards.

Establish the Data Governance Dashboard

Table 13.1 shows an example of controls mapped to regulations, which can be measured to determine adherence and compliance.

Table 13.1: Regulations mapped to data governance controls		
Regulation	**Section**	**Control**
Australia Privacy Act of 1988	Principle 8: Cross-border disclosure of personal information	Restricted Data Movement: Comply with cross-border disclosure of personal information.
German Federal Protection Act – BDSG and VDS	Section 4b: Transfer of personal data abroad and to supranational or international bodies	Restricted Data Movement: Comply with restrictions on transfer of Germany personal data outside the country, and use by Federal public authorities, public authorities in each German State, and by private bodies.
Personal Data Ordinance, Hong Kong	Chapter 486, Section 33: Prohibition against transfer of personal data to places outside Hong Kong except in specified circumstances	Data Masking: Customer and Employee data elements must be masked before leaving country.
EU GDPR	Recital 30: Device identifiers	Data Collection: Obtain user consent before placing web cookies on user devices.

Figure 13.4 shows how measures are associated with controls for GDPR in Collibra Data Governance Center. For example, the control "Retention periods for Customer Data" is measured by "% of Customer opportunities where the retention policies are being followed."

Figure 13.5 shows an example of the overall adherence of controls implemented for GDPR Article 5 (Principles related to processing of personal data). In this example, only one metric is associated with each control, and each metric is weighted equally. For example, the control "Retention periods for Customer Data" is measured by "% of Customer Data opportunities where the retention policies are being followed."

Data Entity	Dimension	Rows Passed	Rows Failed	Quality Score	Result
ⅴ GDPR		640.0	160.0	80.0	✗
ⅴ Retention periods for Customer Data		50.0	50.0	50.0	✗
% of Customer Data opportunities where the retention policies are being followed	Article 5 ✗	50.0	50.0	50.0	✗
ⅴ Customer data is traced within data flows		90.0	10.0	90.0	✓
% of Customer Data traced with data lineage to the Authoritative System of Record	Article 30 ✗	90.0	10.0	90.0	✓
ⅴ Periodic data quality checks		95.0	5.0	95.0	✓
% of timely Data Quality Checks	Article 5 ✗	95.0	5.0	95.0	✓
ⅴ Approval of customer data collection		80.0	20.0	80.0	✗
% of Approvals taken before customer data collection	Article 5 ✗	80.0	20.0	80.0	✗
ⅴ Metadata integration		60.0	40.0	60.0	✗
% of Allowable values for Customer and Employee Data cataloged in the reference data ...	Article 30 ✗	60.0	40.0	80.0	✗
ⅴ Data lineage for sensitive data		85.0	15.0	85.0	✓
% of Sensitive Data tagged in data lineage to the Authoritative System of Record	Article 30 ✗	85.0	15.0	85.0	✓
ⅴ Data Issue Resolution		90.0	10.0	90.0	✓
% of resolved Data Issues	Article 5 ✗	90.0	10.0	90.0	✓
ⅴ Acceptable Use		90.0	10.0	90.0	✓
% of Data Acceptable Use Agreements executed successfully	Article 5 ✗	90.0	10.0	90.0	✓

Figure 13.4: Data controls mapped to measures in Collibra

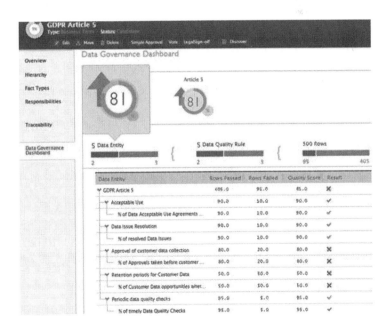

Figure 13.5: GDPR data dashboard—Article 5 controls and measures in Collibra

Figure 13.6 shows an example of rolling up multiple control metrics, (GDPR articles 5 and 30) and how measures are associated with controls for GDPR in Collibra Data Governance Center.

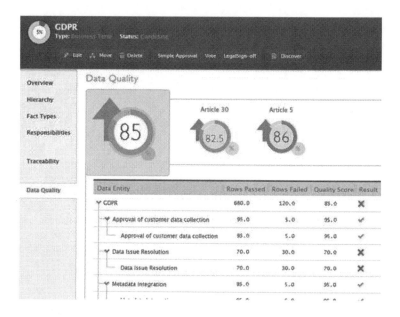

Figure 13.6: Data dashboard for GDPR – Articles 5 and 30 rollup in Collibra

Circulate the Data Governance Dashboard on a Periodic Basis

The data governance dashboard should be generated on a monthly or quarterly basis. The dashboard ought to be circulated to various stake-holders, including the data governance council, stewardship working groups, data owners, data stewards, IT, legal, and compliance stakeholders. A collaborative effort is required to help resolve outstanding questions and to highlight and address key areas for improvement.

Proactive Enforcement Through Audits

Best practices show that optimal data sovereignty programs prepare for regulatory audits. After all, the governing bodies have a personal stake in ensuring that published law, rules, and regulations are followed.

Organizations should involve internal audit teams to take part in periodic monitoring and testing of standards and controls from a data governance, legal, and compliance view to ensure compliance and proper enforcement of data sovereignty laws.

Artifacts from internal testing can be gathered and stored for reporting purposes to show upward compliance progress and allow individualized business action plans to close gaps in processes or strengthen weaknesses. The data protection officer should also be involved in the review of audit results to keep abreast of compliance shortcomings throughout the organization.

Non-Compliance Penalties and Fines

Non-compliance with data sovereignty regulations is not an option, and feigning ignorance is not defensible. Aside from organizations potentially receiving governmental subpoenas from the foreign countries where information is hosted, many regulations empower the data subjects to pursue and win lawsuits against organizations. These stringent regulations, when disregarded, come with substantial consequences, such as compensation for victims and increased company liabilities.

According to the Data Protection Act (DPA) in France, the French Data Protection Authority may choose to impose press sanctions and make an organization's non-compliance public at the expense of those sanctioned or assess pecuniary penalties up to €3M and jail time. In Canada, the Personal Information Protection and Electronic Documents Act (PIPEDA) gives federal courts the power to order organizations to correct practices of non-compliance as well as award damages, including damages for humiliation, with no ceiling. Many organizations have been feverishly preparing for the updated EU GDPR; the associated non-compliance fines for GDPR are listed as the higher of €20M or 4 percent of the organization's worldwide revenues.

By searching the internet, one is able to find several examples of large companies that have violated data sovereignty regulations in one country or another and are suffering the consequences.

Germany Data Fines

In a June 6, 2016, press release, the Data Protection Authority (DPA) of Hamburg, Germany, announced that three fining decisions it had issued against companies unlawfully relying on the invalidated U.S.–EU Safe Harbor Framework (Safe Harbor) had become final. The Hamburg

DPA concluded that after the invalidation of the former U.S.-EU Safe Harbor Framework by the European Court of Justice in October 2015, the companies had failed to otherwise adequately ensure the protection of employee and customer data transferred from Europe to the United States. At least two of the fined companies were not typical "data-related" businesses; addressees of the fining decisions were consumer goods manufacturer Unilever (€11,000), software company Adobe Systems, Inc. (€8,000), and fruit juice maker Punica, a subsidiary of PepsiCo, Inc. (€9,000). The issued fines were relatively low. However, Mr. Johannes Caspar, director of the Hamburg DPA, underlined that the fact that the companies had implemented standard contractual clauses (SCCs) after the start of the investigations had been taken into account in their favor when determining the fine amount. This example confirms the need for companies that relied on Safe Harbor in the past to ensure they install other safeguards, in particular standard contractual clauses.[1,2]

France Data Fines

In January 2014, Google, Inc., was fined €150,000 for various violations of the DPA (such as failure to provide complete notice to data subjects). This is the highest fine imposed by the Commission Nationale de l'Informatique et des Libertés (CNIL) to date.

In August 2014, the CNIL issued a public warning against the French telecommunications service provider Orange for having failed to ensure the security and confidentiality of its customers' personal data. In April 2014, Orange notified the CNIL of a data security breach due to a technical failure of one of its data processors. Orange was sanctioned, in particular, for not having carried out a security audit of the application developed by the data processor before using that application.

In November 2015, the CNIL imposed a fine of €50,000 on Optical Center, a distributor of optical products, for violations related to the security and confidentiality of its customers' personal data.[3]

---

[1] Crowell Morning, "German Data Protection Authority Fines Three Companies for U.S. Data Transfers," June 8, 2016, https://www.crowell.com/NewsEvents/AlertsNewsletters/All/German-Data-Protection-Authority-Fines-Three-Companies-for-US-Data-Transfers.
[2] Hamburg Commissioner for Data Protection and Freedom of Information, "Press Release: Inadmissible Data Transfer to the USA," June 6, 2016, https://www.crowell.com/files/20160606-Press-Release-Inadmissible-Data-Transer-to-the-USA.pdf.
[3] International Comparative Legal Guides, "France: Data Protection 2016," https://www.iclg.co.uk/practice-areas/data-protection/data-protection-2016/france.

Spain Data Fines

The Spanish Agency for Data Protection (AEPD) announced in October 2010 that it had filed a lawsuit against Google for allegedly violating the country's data protection laws. In a statement posted on its website, the Spanish agency claimed that Google illegally gathered data from internet users as it collected images for its Google® Street View™ mapping services. The charges followed an investigation the AEPD launched in May 2010, which the agency said provided evidence of five separate violations committed by Google. These involved the collection and storage of data from internet users connected to Wi-Fi networks as Google took photographs for its Street View service and the transfer of this data to the United States.[4] The AEPD submitted the evidence to a court in Madrid. Google was ultimately fined $1.2 million (€900,000) and ordered to fall in line with the country's data protection rules without delay. Google's Street View mapping service provides real-life images at various locations around the world. But the collection of this data triggered concerns over possible privacy violations. Google acknowledged that its picture-taking vehicles had accidentally captured data from unsecured Wi-Fi systems; Google does not provide users enough information about the personal information it collects and the purposes it uses it for; Google keeps the data for periods longer than permitted under local data laws.[5]

Russia Data Fines

On November 17, 2016, Russian internet service providers (ISPs) were ordered to block public access to LinkedIn following a court ruling that found the social network guilty of violating data laws. Russian law, as reported by Reuters, requires websites that store citizens' personal data to do so on local servers. But the U.S.-based business network—which boasts more than 6 million registered users in Russia—does not do so, said watchdog Roskomnadzor. LinkedIn was expected to go dark in the country by the end of the week; one ISP, Rostelcom, had already blocked access to the site.[6,7]

---

[4] "Spain Sues Google for Violation of Data Protection Laws," redOrbit (October 19, 2010), http://www.redorbit.com/news/technology/1933212/spain_sues_google_for_violation_of_data_protection_laws.

[5] "Spain Privacy Watchdog Fines Google for Breaking Data Law," Reuters (December 19, 2013), http://uk.reuters.com/article/us-spain-google-privacy-idUKBRE9BI12Z20131219.

[6] Tom Brant, "Russia Bans LinkedIn for Violating Data Protection Laws," PC Magazine (November 17, 2016), http://www.pcmag.com/news/349519/russia-to-ban-linkedin-for-violating-data-protection-laws.

Summary

Personal information sent outside a home country is subject to laws in the country to where it is being sent. Organizations must be able to demonstrate an ability to comply with these regulations; provide evidence that processes are implemented, monitored, and enforced; and acknowledge and show their ability to mitigate data breaches. Best practices show that optimal data sovereignty programs use mechanisms such as data dashboards to monitor compliance and prepare for regulatory audits. After all, the governing bodies have a personal stake in ensuring that published law, rules, and regulations are followed. Non-compliance with data sovereignty regulations is not an option, and feigning ignorance is not defensible.

---

[7] Maria Tsvetkova and Andrew Osborn, "Russia Starts Blocking LinkedIn Website After Court Ruling," Reuters (November 17, 2016), http://www.reuters.com/article/us-russia-linkedin-idUSKBN13C0RN.

14

Data Sovereignty in the Cloud

Regulation sample	Description
Australia Privacy Act of 1988, Principle 8.1	Cross-border disclosure of personal information— "Before an APP entity discloses personal information about an individual to a person (the overseas recipient): (a) who is not in Australia or an external Territory; and (b) who is not the entity or the individual; the entity must take such steps as are reasonable in the circumstances to ensure that the overseas recipient does not breach the Australian Privacy Principles. . . ."
German Federal Data Protection Act, Section 4b(3)	Transfer of personal data abroad and to supranational or international bodies— ". . .The adequacy of the afforded level of protection shall be assessed in the light of all circumstances surrounding a data transfer operation or a category of data transfer operations; particular consideration shall be given to the nature of the data, the purpose, the duration of the proposed processing operation, the country of origin, the recipient country and the legal norms, professional rules, and securities measures which apply to the recipient."
Russian Federation – Federal Law 242-FZ (Law 242) of July 21, 2014, on Amending Some Legislative Acts of the Russian Federation in As Much As It Concerns Updating the Procedure for Personal Data Processing in Information-Telecommunication Networks	Obligations of an operator in collecting personal data— ". . .While collecting personal data, for instance by means of the information-telecommunication network "Internet," the operator shall ensure the recording, systematizing, accumulating, storing, making more precise (updating, modifying), and retrieving of the personal data of citizens of the Russian Federation by means of databases located on the territory of the Russian Federation, except for the cases mentioned in Items 2, 3, 4, 8 of Part 1 of Article 6 of the present Federal Law.[1]"

Continued

[1] "Federal Law 242-FZ of July 21, 2014," amendment to Federal Law No. 152-FZ of July 27, 2006, http://wko.at/ooe/Branchen/Industrie/Zusendungen/FEDERAL%20LAW2.pdf.

Regulation sample	Description
People's Republic of China Cybersecurity Law Article 31 and Article 9	Data localization requirement— Effective in June 2017, companies operating in China must store any "personal information and other important data" gathered in-country on servers physically located within mainland China and employ only technology deemed "secure." Any data that needs to be transferred for any business purposes will require governmental permission.
Singapore Personal Data Protection Act, Act 26	Transfer of personal data outside Singapore— "An organization shall not transfer any personal data to a country or territory outside Singapore except in accordance with requirements prescribed under this act. . . ."

As organizations look to leverage the cloud for more of their data computing needs, data distribution, and application hosting, they must understand the ramifications their business and IT decisions could have with respect to data sovereignty laws.

Data Processing, Storage, and Transfers in the Cloud

It can be very compelling to give your data to a managed services provider operating in the cloud to save data storage and data processing costs and increase efficiencies in scaling and standardizing your business and IT needs. The ability to overcome the constraints of geographical borders for quickly processing and sharing data across the globe has been a real gain. However, you need to have a very clear picture of where and how your data will be handled once it leaves its local source and is uploaded.

When you entrust your data to a service provider in the cloud, do you know where your data will physically reside? There is a very good chance it might be stored in a different country from where it was created. Cloud storage services such as Box®, Dropbox™, Google Drive™, IDrive®, Mega, and Microsoft OneDrive®, among others, could be storing your personal data outside its country of origin. Different countries have different laws governing the access to managed services–provided cloud data. It is critical to understand which legal jurisdictions your data is processed, stored, and transmitted in as well as the impact the laws of those jurisdictions may have on the privacy, protection, and availability of information. Data falling into the hands of someone in a different jurisdiction could pose serious issues.

In October 2016, the European Court of Justice issued a judgment declaring the U.S.–EU Safe Harbor Framework an invalid mechanism for complying with EU data protection requirements when transferring personal data from the European Union to the United States. In the meantime, many countries are continuing to take a strong stance on where data can be captured, used, and stored. The table at the start of this chapter mentions some of those regulations. The main reason for this type of data sovereignty legislation stems from countries' concerns that personal data stored outside a person's country of residence may be subject to exposure and the international laws applicable to where the data is being sent, which may be less strict in terms of safeguarding personal information. Furthermore, no one wants to get involved in cross-border conflicts over acknowledgment and recognition of data protection policies or having data subpoenaed.

Microsoft Corp. v. United States

In December 2013, as part of a narcotics trafficking investigation being conducted by the U.S. Federal Bureau of Investigation (FBI), a New York district court judge issued a warrant asking Microsoft to produce all emails and private information associated with a certain account hosted by Microsoft. The account's emails were stored on a server located in Dublin, Ireland—one of many data centers held by Microsoft around the world to improve the speed of service it provides its non-U.S. customers. Microsoft furnished account information kept on its U.S. servers, but it refused to turn over the emails, arguing that a U.S. judge has no authority to issue a warrant for information stored abroad.[2]

Microsoft unsuccessfully challenged the warrant before both a federal magistrate and the District Court for the Southern District of New York. In September 2015, the U.S. Court of Appeals for the Second Circuit heard Microsoft's appeal and in July 2016 ruled unanimously in favor of Microsoft. In October 2016, the U.S. government filed a petition for rehearing with the Second Circuit.[3]

---

[2] Wikipedia, *Microsoft Corp. v. United States*, https://en.wikipedia.org/wiki/Microsoft_Corp._ v._United_States.
[3] Ibid.

Cloud Computing Strategy

A comprehensive cloud computing strategy requires good planning and a thorough understanding from your managed services cloud provider—knowing what data you collect, where that data will be captured, what countries you operate in, where you will store data, where data will be processed, what data may be transmitted to where, whether data is being replicated to other servers in other countries, and who has access to data in any of those processes. Processes and protocols must be established to meet the needs of regulatory data requirements. As we mentioned in Chapter 13, collaboration between data governance, compliance, legal, and IT teams is critical to carrying this out. The goal is to reduce the potential for a default or breach of data sovereignty regulations. It is recommended that regular assessments be conducted to review requirements and validation of procedures and protocols against those requirements.

Cloud Computing Governance Best Practices

Figure 14.1 presents a number of best practices for governing computing in the cloud for data sovereignty requirements.

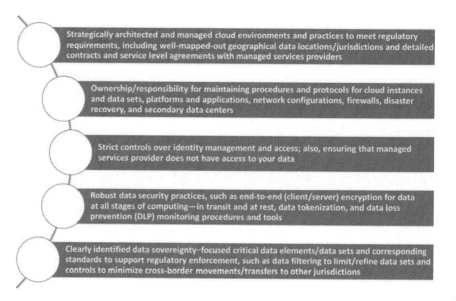

Figure 14.1: Cloud computing best practices

Summary

Data that is stored in a country is subject to the powers of that country—its laws and regulations. To combat the growing trend of cloud computing, countries are enacting data sovereignty legislation to uphold their data protection regulations as they look to protect the privacy rights of their citizens and safeguard their citizens' data no matter where it is. If data is transferred to another country, there is the possibility that it may be subpoenaed by the local government, which may demand access. Businesses need to proactively address the way in which they compute in the cloud and ensure not only that they have transparency of geolocation/jurisdiction of their data, but also that they have adequate controls in place to manage the security and movement of data to adhere to continually developing regulations and to protect against a potential breach or foreign subpoena.

Glossary

Biometrics

Information about an individual that includes identifiers such as fingerprints, retinal scans, and facial recognition.

Cloud computing

Web-based computation that allows for the on-demand sharing of computer processing resources and data. Clouds can be hosted by third parties, shared organizationally, or privately owned.

Content management

The process of digitizing, collecting, and classifying paper and electronic documents.

Controller

The natural or legal person, public authority, agency, or other body that, alone or jointly with others, determines the purposes and means of the processing of personal data. Where the purposes and means of such processing are determined by European Union (EU) or EU member state law, the controller or the specific criteria for its nomination may be provided for by Union or member state law.[1]

Critical data

A set of data or information that is necessary to an organization's operations.

---

[1] GDPR Article 4, "Definitions," http://www.privacy-regulation.eu/en/4.htm.

Critical data elements

In the context of data sovereignty, data elements that may cause significant operational, regulatory, or financial risk if they are not collected or are incorrect, compromised, or used inappropriately.

Critical data sets

In the context of data sovereignty, groupings or collections of data that may cause operational, regulatory, or financial risk if they are not collected or are incorrect, compromised, or used inappropriately.

Data anonymization

The process of removing, scrubbing, and redacting personally identifiable information from data sets in an effort to keep the data subject from being identified.

Data architecture

A discipline that sets data standards for data systems as a vision or a model of the eventual interactions between those data systems.[2]

Data category

Logical classification of information to support data governance.

Data controls

Controls that provide detailed procedures to report regulatory and data governance program adherence. One or more regulations may support each data standard and policy; multiple business terms may also be regulated by these controls.

Data encryption

The process of rendering sensitive data unreadable so that an attacker cannot gain unauthorized access to it.

Data governance

The formulation of policy to optimize, secure, and leverage information as an enterprise asset by aligning the objectives of multiple functions.

Data governance executive

The individual accountable for data governance. The role may be carried out by a company's chief data officer, or, in the case of large

---

[2] Wikipedia, "Data architecture," http://en.wikipedia.org/wiki/Data_architecture.

organizations, there may be multiple data governance executives representing the company's different business units.

Data integration

A process that involves combining data from multiple sources to provide new insights to business users.

Data masking

The process of systematically transforming sensitive information into realistic, but fictionalized, values.

Data modeling

The process of establishing data models, which use a set of symbols and text to precisely explain a subset of real information to improve communication within the organization and thereby lead to a more flexible and stable application environment.[3]

Data owner

A senior leader who is ultimately accountable for the trustworthiness and safeguarding of information within his or her respective domain.

Data ownership and stewardship

The process of identifying individuals who will be accountable for the trustworthiness of data within their purview, as well as for supporting security and privacy.

Data policies

Guidelines that provide a broad framework for how decisions should be made regarding data. Data policies serve as guidelines for the appropriate management of an organization's data. One or more data standards may support each data policy.

Data privacy

The process that involves protecting data belonging to an individual or organization.

Data processes

A set of detailed tasks to implement a data standard, including special instructions for the successful implementation of the data standard.

---

[3] Steve Hoberman, *Data Modeling Made Simple*, 2nd Edition (Technics Publications LLC, 2009).

Data protection impact assessment

An assessment of the impact of processing operations on the protection of personal data (GDPR Article 35). Also refers to tools that help organizations seek, understand, and mitigate privacy issues before the program or new activities have left the ideation phase.

Data protection officer

An individual with strong knowledge of data protection and sovereignty laws who works with executive governance program sponsors, advising on data processing activities, regulatory compliance, and risk avoidance.

Data quality management

A discipline that includes methods to measure and improve the quality and integrity of an organization's data.

Data security

The process of avoiding unauthorized access to data.

Data sovereignty

Privacy legislation that covers information that is subject to the laws of the country in which the information is located or stored. Data sovereignty impacts the protection of data and is affected by governmental regulations for data privacy, data storage, data processing, and data transfers across international borders.

Data standards

High-level statements that provide detailed rules about how to implement data policies. Data standards need more detail before they can be operationalized. One or more data processes may support each data standard.

Data subject

An identifiable natural person; that is, one who can be identified, directly or indirectly, by reference to an identifier such as a name, an identification number, location data, or an online identifier or to one or more factors specific to the physical, physiological, genetic, mental, economic, cultural, or social identity of that natural person.[4]

---

[4] GDPR Article 4, "Definitions."

Data tokenization

The process of substituting a sensitive data element with a non-sensitive equivalent, referred to as a token, that has no extrinsic or exploitable meaning or value. The token is a reference that maps back to the sensitive data through a tokenization system. The mapping from original data to a token uses methods that render tokens infeasible to reverse in the absence of the tokenization system, for example using tokens created from random numbers.

Data warehousing and business intelligence

The process of creating a centralized repository of data for reporting and analysis.

End user computing

Solutions developed outside the information technology environment to fulfill a business, financial, or operational need on a recurring basis. These can be any form of spreadsheets, documents, queries, scripts, and so on.

Enterprise data management (EDM)

The ability of an organization to precisely define, easily integrate, and effectively retrieve data for both internal applications and external communication.[5] EDM includes a number of disciplines, such as data architecture, data modeling, data integration (extract, transform, load, or ETL), data security, data privacy, master data management, reference data management, data warehousing and business intelligence, information lifecycle management, content management, metadata management, data quality management, data ownership and stewardship, and critical data elements and critical data sets. Strictly speaking, data security and privacy are broader disciplines, but they have significant interdependencies with enterprise data management and data governance.

Extract, transform, load (ETL)

A process used in data warehousing to extract data from one or more data sources, transform the data, and load the data into a target database.

---

[5] Wikipedia, "Enterprise data management," http://en.wikipedia.org/wiki/Enterprise_data_management.

Human-generated data

Another term used to describe end user computing; *see* end user computing. Additional examples are voice dictation, email, customer service representative notes, surveys, and electronic medical records.

Information lifecycle management

The process and methodology of managing information through its lifecycle, from creation through disposal, including compliance with legal, regulatory, and privacy requirements.

Internet of things

Refers to physical objects that use an Internet Protocol (IP) address to connect to the internet. Some examples are smartphones, tablets, sensors, and meters. These objects can be wired, wireless, or a combination of both.

Jurisdiction

A geographic location where regulations may apply.

Master data management

The process of establishing a single version of the truth for an organization's critical data entities, such as customers, products, materials, vendors, and chart of accounts.

Metadata management

The management of information that describes the characteristics of any data artifact, such as its name, location, criticality, quality, business rules, and relationships to other data artifacts.

Model acceptable use

A subdiscipline of model governance that includes the permitted uses of a model, including processes to ensure that models are used in a manner consistent with business policies and regulatory requirements.

Model metadata management

A subdiscipline of model governance that includes a comprehensive model catalog, including details regarding name, creation date, methodology, input variables, and output variables.

Model ownership

A subdiscipline of model governance that includes the name of the model owner to enforce accountability for the results of the models.

Model quality management

A subdiscipline of model governance that includes processes to validate the results of models on an ongoing basis.

Personal data

Any information relating to an identified or identifiable natural person ("data subject").[6]

Privacy

The "right to be left alone," as defined in a *Harvard Law Review* article entitled "The Right to Privacy," written in 1890 by Louis Brandeis and Samuel Warren. Subsequent regulations and legislation around the world have built on this definition.

Privacy impact assessment (PIA)

See Data protection impact assessment.

Processor

A natural or legal person, public authority, agency, or other body that processes personal data on behalf of the controller.[7]

Pseudonymization

The process of changing a data subject's name to a false or unrecognizable name.

Reference data management

The process of managing static data such as country codes, state or province codes, and industry classification codes, which may be placed in lookup tables for reference by other applications across the enterprise.

Roskomnadzor

Russia's Data Protection Authority.

Taxonomy

The classification of data into categories.

Unstructured data

Data such as that found in emails, Microsoft Word documents, Microsoft Excel files, and chat logs.

---

[6] GDPR Article 4, "Definitions."
[7] Ibid.

Web cookie

A small piece of data that a website asks a browser to store on the computer or mobile device. The cookie enables the website to "remember" a user's actions or preferences over time.[8]

Web/social media

Technologies that let users share information, pictures, employment opportunities, and other forms of expression through virtual networks and communities. Some examples are Facebook, Instagram®, LinkedIn, Snapchat®, and Twitter.

---

[8] European Commission, Information Providers Guide, The EU Internet Handbook, "Cookies," http://ec.europa.eu/ipg/basics/legal/cookies/index_en.htm.

B

Acronyms

AEPD	Spanish Agency for Data Protection
AML	Anti-Money Laundering
APP	Australian Privacy Principle
BI	Business Intelligence
CASL	Canada's Anti-Spam Law
CDE	Critical Data Element
CFO	Chief Financial Officer
CMS	Centers for Medicare and Medicaid Services (United States)
CNIL	Commission Nationale de l'Informatique et des Libertés (France)
COPPA	Children's Online Privacy Protection Act (United States)
CRO	Chief Risk Officer
DAMA	Data Administration Management Association
DLP	Data Loss Prevention
DPA	Data Protection Act (France)
DPA	Data Protection Authority (Hamburg, Germany)
DPA	Digital Privacy Act (Canada)
DPIA	Data Protection Impact Assessment
DPO	Data Protection Officer
EDM	Enterprise Data Management

EPHI	Electronic Protected Health Information
ETL	Extract, Transform, Load
EU	European Union
EUC	End User Computing
FBI	Federal Bureau of Investigation (United States)
FDA	Food and Drug Administration (United States)
FIPPs	Fair Information Practice Principles
FIPs	Fair Information Practices
FTC	Federal Trade Commission (United States)
GDPR	General Data Protection Regulation (European Union)
HEW	Department of Health, Education, and Welfare (United States)
HIPAA	Health Insurance Portability and Accountability Act of 1996 (United States)
HR	Human Resources
IBM	International Business Machines
IGC	Information Governance Catalog
ILM	Information Lifecycle Management
IoT	Internet of Things
IP	Internet Protocol
ISO	International Organization for Standardization
ISP	Internet Service Provider
IT	Information Technology
KPI	Key Performance Indicator
NAICS	North American Industry Classification System
NIST	National Institute of Standards and Technology (United States)
OAIC	Office of the Australian Information Commissioner
OCTAVE	Operationally Critical Threat, Asset, and Vulnerability Evaluation

OECD	Organization of Economic Cooperation and Development
PCI	Payment Card Industry
PDPA	Personal Data Protection Act (Singapore)
PIA	Privacy Impact Assessment
PII	Personally Identifiable Information
PIN	Personal Identification Number
PIPA	Personal Information Protection Act (South Korea)
PIPEDA	Personal Information Protected and Electronic Documents (Canada)
PRC	People's Republic of China
PUC	Public Utility Commission (California)
SCC	Standard Contractual Clause
SDG&E	San Diego Gas & Electric
SME	Subject Matter Expert
SSN	Social Security Number
SVP	Senior Vice President
UK	United Kingdom
US	United States
VP	Vice President

Regulation References

Regulation	Section	Title
Australian Privacy Act	Principle 1	Open and Transparent Management of Personal information
Australian Privacy Act	Principle 10	Quality of Personal Information
Australian Privacy Act	Principle 11	Security of Personal Information
Australian Privacy Act	Principle 12	Access to Personal Information
Australian Privacy Act	Principle 13	Correction of Solicited Personal Information
Australian Privacy Act	Principle 2	Anonymity and Pseudonymity
Australian Privacy Act	Principle 3	Collection of Personal Information
Australian Privacy Act	Principle 8	Cross Border Disclosure of Personal Information
California Civil Code s. 1747–1748.7, Title 1.3 Credit Cards	Section 1747	Song-Beverly Credit Card Act of 1971
California Civil Code s. 1798.29(a) [agency] and California Civil Code s. 1798.82(a)	1798.82(a)	Accounting of Disclosures [1798.25–1798.29]
California Law	Division 3, Part 4, Title 1.8, Chapter 1, Article 7	Accounting of Disclosures [1798.25–1798.29]
Canada Anti-Spam Law (CASL)	6 (1–3)	Unsolicited Electronic Messages Content of Message Period of Validity of Contact information
Canada CASL	Provision 10	Express Consent Sections 6–8
Canada CASL	Provision 44	Directors and Officers of Corporations
Canada CASL	Provision 17	Notice to Produce

Canada CASL	Provision 40	Enforcement
Canada Personal Information Protected and Electronic Documents (PIPEDA)	Provision 4.7, Principle 7	Safeguards
Canada PIPEDA	Section 1, Subsection 7	Collection Without Knowledge, Use Without Knowledge
Canada PIPEDA	Section 1, Subsection 9	When Access Is Prohibited, Limit
Canada PIPEDA	Section 2, Subsection 12.1	Powers of Commissioner
Canada PIPEDA	Section 2, Subsection 16	Remedies
Canada PIPEDA	Section 3, Subsection 18	Delegation
European Union General Data Protection Regulation (EU GDPR)	Article 16	Right to Rectification
EU GDPR	Article 17	Right to Erasure ("Right to Be Forgotten")
EU GDPR	Article 19	Notification Obligation Regarding Rectification or Erasure of Personal Data or Restriction of Processing
EU GDPR	Article 21	Right to Object
EU GDPR	Article 22	Automated Individual Decision-Making Including Profiling
EU GDPR	Article 30	Records of Processing Activities
EU GDPR	Article 32	Security of Processing
EU GDPR	Article 33	Notification of a Personal Data Breach to the Supervisory Authority
EU GDPR	Article 34	Communication of a Personal Data Breach to the Data Subject
EU GDPR	Article 35	Data Protection Impact Assessment
EU GDPR	Article 37	Designation of the Data Protection Officer
EU GDPR	Article 38	Position of the Data Protection Officer
EU GDPR	Article 40	Codes of Conduct
EU GDPR	Article 44	General Principles for Transfers
EU GDPR	Article 47	Binding Corporate Rules
EU GDPR	Article 50	International Cooperation for the Protection of Personal Data

EU GDPR	Article 6	Lawfulness of Processing
EU GDPR	Article 7	Conditions for Consent
EU GDPR	Article 8	Conditions Applicable to Child's Consent in Relation to Information Society Services
EU GDPR	Article 87	Processing of the National Identification Number
EU GDPR	Article 88	Processing in the Context of Employment
EU GDPR	Article 9	Processing of Special Categories of Personal Data
EU GDPR	Recital 26	Principles of Personal Data Application
EU GDPR	Recital 30	Device Identifiers
EU GDPR	Recital 85	Addressing Personal Data Breach
France Data Protection Act (DPA)	Article 10	Decisions Based on Automated Processing
France DPA	Article 44	Monitoring the Implementation of Treatments
France DPA	Article 8(7)	Statistical Processing
German Federal Data Protection Act	Section 4b	Transfer of Personal Data Abroad and to Supranational or International Bodies
German Federal Data Protection Act	Section 9	Technical and Organizational Measures
Hong Kong Personal Data Privacy Ordinance	Section 22	Data Correction Request
Hong Kong Personal Data Privacy Ordinance	Section 33	Prohibition Against Transfer of Personal Data Except in Specified Circumstances
Irish Data Protection Acts of 1998 and 2003	Section 2	Collection, Processing, Keeping, Use, and Disclosure of Personal Data
Irish Data Protection Acts of 1998 and 2003	Section 9	The Commissioner
Irish Data Protection Acts of 1998 and 2003, Amendment of Section 2 (Biometrics in the Workplace)	Section 2C	Security Measures for Personal Data
Laws of Malaysia Personal Data Act 2010	Act 709, Section 129	Transfer of Personal Data to Places Outside of Malaysia
Laws of Malaysia Personal Data Act 2010	Act 709, Section 44	Record to Be Kept by Data User
The 190th General Court of the Commonwealth of Massachusetts	Part 1, Title XV, Chapter 93H, Section 3	Duty to Report Known Security Breach or Unauthorized Use of Personal Information

People's Republic of China (PRC) Cybersecurity Law Draft	Chapter I, Article 1	This law is formulated so as to ensure network security; to preserve cyberspace sovereignty, national security, and the societal public interest; to protect the lawful rights and interests of citizens, legal persons, and other organizations; and to promote the healthy development of economic and social informatization.
PRC Cybersecurity Law Draft	Chapter I, Article 9	The State protects the rights of citizens, legal persons, and other organizations to use networks in accordance with law; it promotes widespread network access, raises the level of network services, provides secure and convenient network services to society, and guarantees the lawful, orderly, and free circulation of network information. Any person and organization shall, when using the network, abide by the Constitution and laws, observe public order, and respect social morality. They must not endanger network security and must not use the network to engage in activities harming national security, propagating of terrorism and extremism, inciting ethnic hatred and ethnic discrimination, disseminating obscene and sexual information, slandering or defaming others, upsetting social order, harming the public interest, or infringing of other persons' intellectual property or other lawful rights and interests.
PRC Cybersecurity Law Draft	Chapter III, Section 2, Article 31	Critical information infrastructure operators shall store citizens' personal information, and other important data gathered and produced during operations, within the mainland territory of the People's Republic of China; where due to business requirements it is truly necessary to store it outside the mainland or provide it to individuals or organizations outside the mainland, they shall follow the measures jointly formulated by the State network information departments and the relevant departments of the State Council to conduct a security assessment. Where laws or administrative regulations otherwise provide, follow those provisions.
Russian Federal Law 152-FZ	Article 11	Biometric Personal Data
Russian Federal Law 152-FZ	Article 12	Cross-Border Transfer of Personal Data
Russian Federal Law 152-FZ	Article 14	Personal Data Subject's Right to Access His Personal Data
Russian Federal Law 152-FZ	Article 18.1	Measures Aimed at Ensuring the Implementation of Operator Responsibilities Stipulated by This Federal Law

Russian Federal Law 152-FZ	Article 19	Measures to Ensure the Security of Personal Data Processing
Russian Federal Law 152-FZ	Chapter 2, Article 6	The Processing of Personal Data
Singapore Personal Data Protection Act (PDPA)	Act 11	Compliance with Act
Singapore PDPA	Act 22	Correction of Personal Data
Singapore PDPA	Act 23	Accuracy of Personal Data
Singapore PDPA	Act 24	Protection of Personal Data
Singapore PDPA	Act 26	Transfer of Personal Data Outside Singapore
Singapore PDPA	Act 59	Preservation of Secrecy
Singapore PDPA	Second Schedule	Collection of Personal Data Without Consent
South Korea Personal Information Protection Act (PIPA)	Article 24	Limitation to Processing Unique Identifier
U.S. Americans with Disabilities Act, Title III	Subpart B	General Requirements
U.S. Children's Online Privacy Protection Act (COPPA) of 1998	16 CFR Part 312	COPPA imposes certain requirements on operators of websites or online services directed to children under 13 years of age, and on operators of other websites or online services that have actual knowledge that they are collecting personal information online from a child under 13 years of age.
U.S. Civil Rights Act of 1964	Title VII, Section 703	Discrimination Because of Race, Color, Religion, Sex, or National Origin: It shall be an unlawful employment practice for an employer (1) to fail or refuse to hire or to discharge any individual, or otherwise to discriminate against any individual with respect to his compensation, terms, conditions, or privileges of employment, because of such individual's race, color, religion, sex, or national origin.
U.S. Department of Commerce Privacy Shield	N/A	Provide companies on both sides of the Atlantic with a mechanism to comply with data protection requirements when transferring personal data from the European Union and Switzerland to the United States in support of transatlantic commerce.
U.S. Equal Credit Opportunity Act	Section 1691	Scope of Prohibition
U.S. Fair Credit Reporting Act	Section 604	Permissible Purposes of Consumer Reports

U.S. Federal Trade Commission Act	Section 5	Unfair Methods of Competition Unlawful; Prevention by Commission
U.S. Food and Drug Administration Code of Federal Regulations Title 21	Part 50, Section 50.20	Protection of Human Subjects – Informed Consent of Human Subjects – General Requirements for Informed Consent

Made in the USA
Columbia, SC
19 March 2019